MW01533715

SOUP
LOVE

Name: Liza Cannata
Title: Soup Love: The art of making everyone's favorite comfort food
Identifiers: ISBN 9798218257422 (hardcover)

Printed in the USA

Design by Alyssa Warnock
Cover photography by Michelle K. Min

To my Mom, the original soup queen.
Thank you for providing a lifetime
of nourishment and comfort.

"Soup is a lot like a family. Each ingredient enhances the others; each batch has its own characteristics; and it needs time to simmer to reach full flavor."

—Marge Kennedy

# SOUP LOVE

## THE ART OF MAKING EVERYONE'S FAVORITE COMFORT FOOD

✳

### LIZA CANNATA

PHOTOS BY MICHELLE K. MIN
FOOD STYLING BY FANNY PAN

# CONTENTS

# SOUP

## MEXICAN

| | |
|---|---|
| Slow Cooker White Bean Chili | 60 |
| Chicken Pozole Verde | 64 |
| Pork Pozole Rojo | 68 |
| Orange October Chicken Tortilla Soup | 73 |
| Easy Black Bean Soup | 77 |
| Albóndigas Soup (Mexican Meatball Soup) | 78 |
| Game Day Turkey Black Bean Chili | 83 |
| Quinoa Chili | 84 |

## VEGETARIAN & VEGAN

| | |
|---|---|
| Butternut Squash, Brown Rice & Mushroom Soup | 89 |
| Corn Soup | 90 |
| Curried Sweet Potato Soup | 93 |
| Detox Lentil & Split Pea Soup | 94 |
| Super Green Alkalizing Soup | 97 |
| Spring Asparagus Soup | 98 |
| Butternut Squash Soup | 101 |
| Spring Green Minestrone with Pesto | 102 |
| Green or Red Lentil Curry | 105 |
| Pea Soup | 106 |
| Carrot Soup | 109 |
| Zucchini, Cauliflower & Leek Soup | 110 |
| Chickpea & Kale Stew | 113 |
| Cauliflower Soup with Grilled Cheese Croutons | 114 |

# INTRODUCTION

After writing a book on salads, it was only fitting that I tackle salad's partner for my next book: SOUP. To me, soup is so much more than a dish. It is family. It is friends. It is coming together. It is warming and nourishing. Soup is LOVE.

As cliché as it sounds, my childhood is filled with memories of my Jewish mother making chicken soup. From the large pot of vegetables and chicken parts bubbling on the stove, to the familiar aroma wafting through the house, and the giant bowls of broth chilling in our fridge, soup-making is ingrained in my soul. Good news, bad news, my mom made soup. And to this day, the minute she hears that someone is struggling, she brings out her big stock pot. To know soup is to know my mother. Dynamic, yet simple. Authentic and practical. Comforting, nurturing, and always aiming to please.

Everyone loves soup and fortunately, I love making soup. Almost every week I make a big pot of soup, from hearty meat soups in the winter to light vegan purees in the warmer months. One of my favorite things about soup is that it is easy. It can be made ahead of meal time (in fact, most even taste better the day after making it as the flavors settle) and it is almost always made in one pot. Plus, soup is extremely flexible and versatile. Add an ingredient, forget an ingredient...it will most likely always turn out delicious. Healthy, easy and forgiving, it is foolproof!

This book is a collection of my favorite, surefire soup recipes, ranging from family classics, traditional recipes, and favorites from around the world. It offers fresh inspiration and creative options for all the soup lovers out there.

# WHY SOUP?

From a holistic nutrition perspective, soup is an absolute must-have for a healthy diet. It is packed with all the essential vitamins, minerals, and antioxidants that your body craves. Additionally, soup is high in fiber, typically containing ingredients such as whole grains, legumes, and vegetables. Adequate dietary fiber not only supports digestive health but also aids in weight management and helps regulate blood sugar levels. The best part? Soup is incredibly satisfying and filling, all while being low in calories and fat.

However, it's important to note that not all soups are created equal. Just like salads, the nutritional value of soups can vary depending on the ingredients used. Some canned or store-bought varieties can be high in sodium, unhealthy fats, or added sugars. But when you make your own homemade soup using fresh, whole ingredients, you can be certain that you are nourishing your body in the best way possible.

Considering all of these notable health benefits, it is no wonder that soup is one of the oldest traditional meals in the world. In fact, almost all cultures have a form of soup deeply embedded in their cuisine. Soup Love is an exploration of the diverse culture of soup, celebrating the unique flavors, ingredients, and cooking methods from around the world.

**Italian** From Minestrone and Italian Wedding Soup to Ribollita, Italians have mastered some of the best soups in the world. Known for their simplicity and using only fresh, seasonal ingredients, these soups are delicious, pure and full of flavor.

**Mexican** From authentic pozole to Tex-Mex chili, Mexican inspired soups and stews are always a winner. Made with traditional Mexican ingredients like beans, rice, garlic, chili powder, and oregano, they are full of the Mexican flavors we all love. Flavor-packed and satisfying, this is easily my favorite category of soups. Spice level is always adjustable.

**Vegan & Vegetarian** This section includes a collection of vegetable based soups that are just as healthy as they are tasty. These soups are cleansing, alkalizing and easy to digest. They are all vegetarian if made with vegetable stock and can all be made vegan by using olive oil instead of butter and omitting the dairy garnishes.

**Asian-Inspired** soups are a delicious and nourishing option that can be enjoyed in a range of different ways. From Japanese ramen, to Vietnamese pho, Chinese wonton and Thai curry, they typically feature a variety of ingredients such as vegetables, spices, noodles and protein and are characterized by their bold and complex flavors.

**Comfort** This is a collection of family classics and traditional recipes that nourish the heart and the soul. They are rich, hearty and healing, often full of familiar flavors that offer emotional comfort. Like Nana's Beef and Barley and Mom's Chicken Noodle, these are recipes that have been passed down through generations and bring back positive memories and emotional connections.

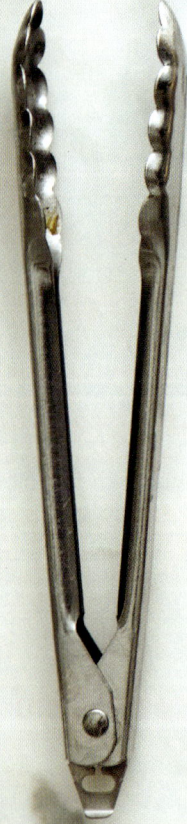

# TIPS & TOOLS

From my years of experience making soup, I have found that a few simple tips and the right tools make all the difference. Here is my behind the scenes list of these soup making pearls of wisdom.

**PANTRY**

**TOOLS**

**MAKING STOCK**

**SOAKING BEANS**

# PANTRY

A well-stocked pantry is essential to making a great soup. When you have high-quality, fresh ingredients at your disposal, meal preparation is simple. By stocking my pantry and refrigerator with "soup staples," it is super easy to throw together a delicious soup. From beans, pasta and grains, to spices and condiments, these basics are an integral part of every soup.

The following is a comprehensive list of the pantry ingredients you will need to make all of the recipes in this book. You can find most of these items at your local grocery store. Always try to buy organic, when possible. And, make sure to always save your Parmesan rinds! They are often overlooked, but when added to the right soup, they create a special rich, deep flavor that's impossible to resist.

## Oils
Extra virgin olive oil
Sesame oil
Toasted sesame oil
Canola oil
Olive oil cooking spray
Grapeseed oil

## Condiments
Soy sauce or tamari
Sriracha
Honey
Maple syrup
Sugar (white and brown)
Red curry paste
Fish sauce
Pesto
Apple cider vinegar
White vinegar
Tomato paste
White wine for cooking
Red wine for cooking

## Cheese & Dairy
Parmesan cheese, grated,
    shaved, wedge, and rinds
Cotija cheese
Shredded Jack cheese
Cream
Milk

## Spices + Dried Goods
Sea salt, finely ground
Black peppercorns
Red pepper flakes
Sesame seeds
Chili Powder
Ground cumin
Dried oregano
Bay leaves
Dried beans
    (white, black, pinto)
Canned beans
    (white, black, pinto)
Breadcrumbs
White rice
Rice noodles
Ramen noodles

# TOOLS

### Knives
High quality, sharp knives are essential. I would recommend the following: a chef's knife, a serrated bread knife and a paring knife.

### Knife Sharpener
I use a manual handheld sharpener every couple of months. If you prefer to have someone else do the sharpening, most high-end groceries and farmer's markets have a knife sharpener available.

### Cutting Boards
Two or three wooden cutting boards for fruits and vegetables. A plastic, dishwasher safe board reserved for meat and fish to avoid cross contamination.

### Stock Pot
12 or 16-quart stainless steel or an enamel stock pot with a lid to make broths and stocks.

### Dutch Oven
A 7-quart dutch oven is my preferred soup vessel. I also have a 4-quart for smaller batches. It's worth it to invest in a Le Creuset or Staub.

### Crock Pot

### Vegetable Peeler

### Handheld Strainer

### Large Strainer

### Vitamix or Immersion Blender

### Glass Nesting Bowls

### Mason Jars or Silicone Food Storage Bags
8oz and 16oz glass for storing and freezing soup and stocks.

### Citrus Juicer/Reamer

### Microplane Zester/Cheese Grater

### Tongs

### Egg Slicer

### Pepper Grinder

### Scissors
I use my scissors to snip herbs for garnish.

# MAKING STOCK

Homemade stock is infinitely more nutritious and delicious than anything available in a box or can at the grocery store. It is full of vitamins and minerals that the body can easily process and assimilate. Homemade stock is also deeper, richer, and more complex than store bought, serving as a more flavorful base for soups and stews. It really is the key to making a good soup.

Besides time, making homemade stock is relatively easy. I usually make a big batch and store it in the freezer in pre-measured mason jars, making sure to leave room at the top for the liquid to expand without shattering the glass. It defrosts easily in a bowl of warm water or in the fridge overnight. You can also store the stock in ziplock bags and lay them flat on a baking sheet in the freezer to save on space. The following section outlines all the essential stock recipes you will need for the soups in this book: beef, chicken, vegetable and seafood. Each method is made in a large stockpot, but you can easily throw everything in a slow cooker and cook on low for 6 to 8 hours.

# CHICKEN STOCK

1 (4-pound) whole organic chicken or
    3 to 4 pounds mixed chicken parts
2 large yellow onions, unpeeled and quartered
6 garlic cloves, crushed with the back of knife
4 large carrots, unpeeled and quartered
2 parsnips, unpeeled and halved crosswise
6 celery stalks with leaves, quartered
1 bunch parsley
2 bay leaves
2 teaspoons black peppercorns
2 teaspoons sea salt
1 tablespoon vinegar (apple cider or white)

Place the chicken, onions, garlic, carrots, parsnips, celery, parsley, bay leaves, peppercorns, salt and vinegar in a large stockpot. Add enough water to completely cover the chicken and vegetables by 1 to 2 inches. Bring the liquid to a boil and remove the scum that rises to the top. Reduce the heat to low and simmer, uncovered, for 4 to 8 hours. The longer you cook the stock, the richer it will be. Once done, carefully strain the stock through a fine-mesh strainer into a large bowl (or bowls), let cool, and refrigerate until completely chilled, about 6 hours or overnight. Discard the solids. Skim off and discard any fat that has solidified on the surface. Pack the stock in containers and refrigerate up to 5 days or freeze for up to 6 months.

# BEEF STOCK

5 pounds meaty beef bones, including
   a marrow bone
2 large yellow onions, peeled and roughly
chopped
4 large carrots, unpeeled and quartered
4 celery stalks with leaves, quartered
1 cup dry red wine
1 (6-ounce) can tomato paste
6 garlic cloves, unpeeled
1 bunch parsley
3 bay leaves
1 small bunch thyme
2 teaspoons black peppercorns
2 teaspoons sea salt
1 tablespoon vinegar (apple cider or white)

Preheat the oven to 425 degrees. Place the beef bones, onions, carrots, and celery on a large roasting pan and roast, turning occasionally, until well browned, about 45 minutes. Remove the bones and vegetables and place them in a large stockpot and set aside. Drain off all but 2 tablespoons of fat in the roasting pan and place it on the stovetop on medium heat (will cover 2 burners). Add the wine to the roasting pan and deglaze the pan, using a metal spatula to scrape up all of the browned bits stuck to the bottom of the pan. Carefully, add the mixture to the stockpot. Add the tomato paste, garlic, herbs, peppercorns, salt and vinegar. Add enough water to completely cover the bones and vegetables by 1 to 2 inches.

Bring the liquid to a boil, reduce to a simmer and cook for 4 to 6 hours, skimming the top occasionally. Remove from heat and discard most of the bones (this makes it easier strain). Carefully strain the stock through a fine-mesh strainer into a large bowl (or bowls), let cool, and refrigerate until completely chilled, about 6 hours or overnight. Discard the solids. Skim off and discard any fat that has solidified on the surface. Pack the stock in containers and refrigerate up to 5 days or freeze for up to 6 months.

# SEAFOOD STOCK

1 tablespoon olive oil

1 ½ pounds shellfish shells, from
    shrimp, lobster, and/or crab

1 large yellow onion, peeled and
    roughly chopped

2 carrots, unpeeled and quartered

3 celery stalks with leaves, quartered

3 garlic cloves, peeled and roughly chopped

½ cup dry white wine

2 tablespoons tomato paste

4 sprigs thyme

2 teaspoons black peppercorns

2 teaspoons sea salt

Heat olive oil in a large stock pot over medium heat. Add the shellfish shells, onions, carrots, and celery and sauté until lightly browned, about 10 minutes. Add the garlic and cook for 1 more minute. Add the remaining stock ingredients and 6 cups of filtered water. Bring the mixture to a boil, reduce the heat to low and simmer, uncovered, for 1 to 2 hours. Carefully strain the stock through a fine-mesh strainer into a large bowl and let cool. Discard the solids. Transfer to containers and refrigerate up to 3 days or freeze for up to 6 months.

# VEGETABLE STOCK

1 tablespoon olive oil

2 large yellow onions, unpeeled and quartered

6 large carrots, unpeeled and quartered

6 celery stalks with leaves, quartered

2 leeks, washed and quartered

1 pound cremini mushrooms, halved

1 head garlic, unpeeled and halved crosswise

1 bunch parsley

1 small bunch of thyme

2 bay leaves

2 teaspoons black peppercorns

2 teaspoons sea salt

1 tablespoon apple cider vinegar

Optional extras: fennel, turnips, parsnips

Heat olive oil in a large stock pot over medium heat. Add the onions, carrots, celery, and leeks and sauté for 5 minutes. Add the remaining stock ingredients and 8 cups of filtered water. Bring the mixture to a boil, reduce the heat to low and simmer, uncovered, for 1 to 2 hours. Carefully strain the stock through a fine-mesh strainer into a large bowl and let cool. Discard the solids. Transfer to containers and refrigerate up to 5 days or freeze for up to 6 months.

# SOAKING BEANS

Many recipes in this book call for beans. Like making stock, homemade beans are notably tastier and healthier than canned varieties. Of course, a soup will still be plenty delicious if you use canned beans, but if you have the time, it is worth it to go the extra mile. The main drawback to making beans from scratch is remembering to soak the dried beans in water ahead of time. The reason for this is twofold: one, it makes them more digestible by breaking down some of the complex sugars and two, it cuts cooking time in half. There are two methods to soak dried beans:

## THE OVERNIGHT SOAK

Rinse the beans in a colander, removing any small rocks or debris.

Place the beans in a large stockpot and cover with 2 inches of water.

Cover the stockpot and soak for 8 to 12 hours.

Drain the soaked beans in a colander, discarding the soaking water.

## THE QUICK-SOAK

Rinse the beans in a colander, removing any small rocks or debris.

Place the beans in a large stock pot and cover them with water and bring to a boil for 3 minutes.

Remove from heat, cover, and let the beans sit for at least 1 hour.

Drain the soaked beans in a colander, discarding the soaking water.

Once either soaking method is complete, place the soaked beans back in the large stockpot and cover them with 2 inches of cold water. Bring the water to a boil, skim any foam that rises to the surface and reduce the heat to a simmer. When the beans have simmered for about 40 minutes, season them with 1 tablespoon of salt. Test the beans and continue cooking until the beans are tender, adding more water if necessary. The cooking time will vary depending on the size and freshness of your beans. I check them every 15 minutes. Once done, drain the beans in a colander and they are ready to use. Some recipes call for using the cooking liquid so make sure to reserve it if necessary.

# ITALIAN

# ITALIAN WEDDING SOUP

Serves 6

Although the name of this soup may suggest that it is a dish typically served at Italian weddings, it is in fact an ancient Neapolitan soup known as "minestra maritata," meaning "married soup," rather than wedding soup. The term "married" refers to the combination of flavors and ingredients, not individuals. Italian wedding soup is a delightful one-pot dish consisting of succulent meatballs, vegetables, and pasta cooked in a delicious and savory broth.

## For the meatballs:
1 pound ground chicken, turkey, pork or beef
   (or a combination)
½ cup breadcrumbs
2 garlic cloves, peeled and minced
2 tablespoons chopped fresh parsley leaves
½ cup freshly grated parmesan,
   plus extra for serving
2 tablespoons milk
1 large egg, lightly beaten
1 teaspoon salt
Freshly ground black pepper

## For the soup:
2 tablespoons good olive oil
1 yellow onion, minced
3 carrots, peeled and diced
3 celery stalks, diced
½ teaspoon salt
Freshly ground pepper
½ cup dry white wine
4 cups chicken stock
1 cup dry small pasta such as orzo
   or acini di pepe
8 ounces baby spinach, washed

✳

*Pro Tip!*

To make this gluten-free,
use gluten-free breadcrumbs
and pasta, or rice

Preheat the oven to 400 degrees. Line a baking sheet with parchment paper. Place the ground meat, breadcrumbs, garlic, parsley, parmesan, milk, egg, salt, and ¼ teaspoon of fresh black pepper in a large bowl and mix gently until just combined. Do not overmix.

Using wet hands, roll the mixture into 1-inch balls and place them onto the prepared baking sheet. Bake until cooked through and lightly browned, about 15 to 20 minutes. Set aside.

In the meantime, for the soup, heat the olive oil over medium heat in a large soup pot. Add onions and cook over medium-low heat until the onions are soft and translucent, about 6 minutes. Add the carrots, celery, salt, and pepper and sauté until softened, about 5 to 6 minutes, stirring occasionally. Add the wine and cook for a couple more minutes. Add the chicken stock, bring the mixture to a boil and reduce to a simmer and cook for 20 minutes.

Cook the pasta in a separate pot according to package directions. Drain and add to soup. Add the meatballs to the soup and simmer for a few minutes. Taste and adjust seasonings. Stir in the fresh spinach and cook for 1 minute, until the spinach is just wilted. Ladle into soup bowls and serve with grated parmesan.

# RIBOLLITA

Serves 6-8

Ribollita is a traditional and hearty Tuscan soup that features vegetables, white beans, and bread. The term "ribollita" translates to "reboiled" in Italian, as it was traditionally prepared by reheating or reboiling leftover vegetable soup and incorporating stale bread. Interestingly, this soup tends to thicken and develop even more flavor the following day, making it a delightful option that can be enjoyed for up to four days when stored in the refrigerator.

2 tablespoons olive oil

1 large yellow onion, diced

3 carrots, diced

3 celery stalks, diced

3 garlic cloves, minced

1 teaspoon sea salt

½ teaspoon freshly ground black pepper

¼ teaspoon red pepper flakes

1 (15-ounce) can chopped tomatoes, preferably San Marzano

1 bunch Tuscan kale, center ribs removed, leaves chopped

1 bay leaf

6 cups chicken stock

1 Parmesan rind, optional

2 (15-ounce) cans white beans (great northern, cannellini), drained and rinsed, or 1 ½ cup dried beans, soaked and cooked plus 1 cup reserved cooking liquid

2 to 3 cups cubed day-old or stale Italian-style bread

½ cup freshly grated parmesan, for serving

Heat the olive oil in a large stockpot over medium heat. Add onions and cook over medium-low heat until the onions are soft and translucent, about 6 minutes. Add the carrots, celery, garlic, salt, ¼ teaspoon of pepper, and pepper flakes. Cook over medium-low heat, until the vegetables are tender, about 6 minutes.

Add the tomatoes with their juice, kale, bay leaf, stock, and parmesan rind if using, and cook over medium-low heat, stirring occasionally, for another 8 minutes. In the bowl of a food processor or Vitamix, combine about 1 cup of the liquid tomato mixture (or reserved bean cooking liquid if using dried beans) and 1 cup of the white beans. Puree.

Pour the bean puree and the remaining whole beans into the soup and stir to combine. Bring the mixture to a boil, reduce the heat, and simmer for 20 minutes. Add the bread to the soup and simmer for 10 more minutes. Remove from heat and carefully remove the parmesan rind and bay leaf. Taste and adjust seasonings and serve hot in large bowls sprinkled with parmesan and drizzled with olive oil.

# ESCAROLE & WHITE BEAN SOUP

Serves 6-8

Packed with white beans, escarole, and pancetta, this Italian-inspired soup can be served as a hearty main course for dinner or as a satisfying lunch option. To make it vegetarian, the pancetta can easily be excluded without compromising on taste.

1 tablespoon olive oil

4 ounces pancetta or bacon, cut into a ¼-inch dice (optional)

1 yellow onion, chopped

2 celery stalks, diced

2 large garlic cloves, minced

½ teaspoon red pepper flakes

½ teaspoon salt

Freshly ground black pepper

2 (15-ounce) cans white beans (great northern, cannellini) or 1 ½ cups dried beans, soaked and cooked with reserved cooking liquid

4 cups vegetable or chicken stock

1 large head escarole, leaves separated, washed, and roughly chopped

Salt and pepper, to taste

Parmesan, for serving

Heat olive oil in a large soup pot over medium-high heat. Add the pancetta or bacon and cook until just brown, about 5 minutes. Transfer the pancetta to a plate with a slotted spoon and set aside.

Pour off all but 2 tablespoons of cooking fat. Add the onion and cook, stirring occasionally, until soft and translucent, about 6 minutes. Add the celery, garlic, red pepper, salt, and ¼ teaspoon of black pepper, and cook for another 3 minutes. Add the escarole to the pot in batches and cook until just wilted about 2 minutes.

If using homemade beans, pour the reserved bean cooking liquid into a large measuring cup and add enough stock to make 4 cups. If using canned beans, drain, rinse, and use 4 cups stock. Add the beans and the liquid to the pot. Bring to a simmer and cook, partially covered, until slightly thickened, about 20 minutes. Stir in the reserved pancetta, taste and adjust seasonings. Serve in large bowls with a drizzle of good-quality olive oil and grated cheese.

# SPAGHETTI & MEATBALL SOUP

Serves 6-8

This soup offers an Italian-American rendition of a beloved traditional Italian classic. Inspired by my dear friend Alison's Italian Gramma's spaghetti and meatball recipe, this one-pot and incredibly kid-friendly dish transforms the pasta into a delightful soup. The brilliance of this recipe lies in its ability to be prepared in advance, eliminating the need for last-minute pasta boiling or straining. Simply heat it up, and dinner is served!

## For Gramma Marie's Italian meatballs:

½ cup breadcrumbs
¼ cup milk
½ onion, chopped
2 garlic cloves, peeled and minced
2 tablespoons chopped parsley
2 tablespoons basil, finely chopped
½ pound ground beef
½ pound ground pork
½ cup freshly grated parmesan
1 egg, lightly beaten
½ tablespoon ketchup
½ tablespoon tomato paste
1 teaspoon salt
Freshly ground pepper

## For the soup:

2 tablespoons olive oil
1 yellow onion, diced
2 garlic cloves, minced
½ teaspoon salt
Freshly ground pepper
½ teaspoon sugar
1 (28-ounce can) tomato puree
3 cups chicken stock
1 Parmesan rind, optional
1 pound spaghetti, cut in half
Freshly grated parmesan and basil leaves
    for garnish

### Pro Tip!

To make this gluten-free,
use zucchini noodles
..................

Preheat the oven to 400 degrees. Line a baking sheet with parchment paper. In a large mixing bowl add the breadcrumbs and milk and let sit for 5 minutes. Place the onions, garlic, parsley and basil in the bowl of a food processor and pulse until finely chopped. Add to the breadcrumb mixture.

Add the ground beef, ground pork, parmesan, egg, ketchup, tomato paste, salt, and ¼ teaspoon of fresh black pepper and mix gently until just combined. Do not overmix. Using wet hands, roll the mixture into 1-inch balls and place onto the prepared baking sheet. Bake until cooked through and lightly browned, about 15 to 20 minutes. Set aside.

Heat the olive oil in a large soup pot over medium. Once oil shimmers, add onions and sauté until soft, about 5 minutes. Add the garlic and sauté another 2 minutes. Add the salt, pepper, sugar, tomatoes, chicken stock, and parmesan rind if using, and bring soup to a boil. Reduce heat and simmer for 30 minutes.

Meanwhile, cook spaghetti according to package directions, drain and set noodles aside.

When the soup is done simmering, add the pasta and meatballs to the soup. Remove parmesan rind, taste and adjust seasonings and ladle into big bowls and serve with fresh grated parmesan and snips of fresh basil.

# SUMMER MINESTRONE

Serves 6-8

Minestrone is a beloved Italian soup that combines an array of vegetables, beans, and/or pasta. Its versatility and adaptability make it a great option for using up leftover vegetables. During the summer, I prepare this simple, light version, incorporating the abundance of delicious summer veggies. In the winter, I opt for potatoes, cabbage, and green beans instead of zucchini and corn. Prepare a large batch, as this soup can be stored for several days and its flavors improve with time.

2 tablespoons olive oil

1 yellow onion, chopped

2 carrots, peeled and chopped
   into ½-inch pieces

2 celery stalks, chopped

2 garlic cloves, minced

2 medium zucchinis, chopped
   into ½-inch pieces

Kernels from two raw ears of corn

2 tablespoons chopped fresh basil

2 tablespoons chopped fresh parsley

1 teaspoon salt

Freshly ground black pepper

1 (15-ounce) can whole tomatoes or 5 to 6
   large fresh tomatoes

4 cups chicken or vegetable stock

1 (15-ounce) can cannellini beans, drained
   and rinsed

Freshly grated parmesan and basil for garnish

*❋*

*Optional*
Add potatoes, savoy cabbage,
green beans, or 1 cup cooked
small shaped pasta
. . . . . . . . . . . . . . . . . .

Heat the olive oil in a large soup pot over medium-high heat. Add the onions, carrots, and celery and sauté until soft, about 5 minutes. Add garlic and cook for another 2 minutes. Add the zucchini, corn, fresh herbs, salt, and ¼ teaspoon of pepper and sauté until vegetables are soft, about 5 to 10 minutes longer. Add a splash of water if the pot gets too dry.

If using fresh tomatoes, remove the skins by placing tomatoes in boiling water for 2 minutes. Once peeled, cut each tomato in half, and gently squeeze out the seeds and chop the flesh. Add to pot. If using canned tomatoes, add tomatoes and juice to the pot, breaking apart tomatoes with your hands, or the back of a wooden spoon.

Add chicken stock and beans and bring the soup to a boil. Reduce to a simmer and cook, partially covered for 20 minutes. Taste and adjust seasonings.

To serve, ladle into big soup bowls, top with freshly grated parmesan and snips of basil.

# TOMATO SOUP Nº 1
# (SUMMER ROASTED)

Serves 6

My youngest son, Jake, requests tomato soup and grilled cheese for lunch just about every week. And since he is pretty hard to resist, I usually end up making it for him. During the summer, when tomatoes are at their freshest, I often prepare a roasted tomato variation. However, if I'm short on time or tomatoes are not in season, canned tomato soup works perfectly fine. You can choose to add cream to either version if desired.

3 pounds ripe tomatoes (Roma, Early Girl)
¼ cup plus 2 tablespoons olive oil
1 teaspoon salt
1 teaspoon freshly ground black pepper
2 tablespoons butter
2 yellow onions, roughly chopped
4 garlic cloves, minced
4 cups vegetable or chicken stock
1 cup basil leaves (packed)
½ cup heavy cream, optional

*Optional*

Top with freshly chopped basil, croutons, freshly grated parmesan
....................

Preheat the oven to 425 degrees. Line a large baking sheet with parchment paper.

Slice the tomatoes widthwise and gently squeeze out most of the seeds. Place them in a bowl with ¼ cup of the olive oil, season with the salt and pepper and toss well to coat. Spread tomatoes evenly on the prepared baking sheet in a single layer, cut side up, and roast for 40 minutes.

Heat the remaining two tablespoons of olive oil and the butter in a large pot over medium heat. Add the onions and cook until soft, about 5 minutes. Add the garlic and cook for about 2 minutes, until fragrant. Add the stock, basil, and oven-roasted tomatoes (and their juices). Bring to a boil then reduce to a simmer and cook for 40 minutes.

Remove from heat and carefully pour the soup mixture into a Vitamix or high-powered blender and blend until smooth, taking care when blending hot liquids. Return the soup to a clean pot, taste and adjust seasonings. Add cream, if using.

To serve, ladle soup into bowls and add any of the optional toppings, if using.

# TOMATO SOUP Nº 2
# (ANY-TIME CANNED)

Serves 6

4 tablespoons olive oil or butter
  (or a combination)
2 yellow onions, roughly chopped
4 garlic cloves, chopped
2 (28-ounce) cans whole with their juice,
  preferably San Marzano
2 cups chicken stock
¼ teaspoon crushed red pepper flakes
½ tablespoon sugar
½ teaspoon salt
Freshly ground black pepper
½ cup heavy cream, optional

Heat the olive oil and/or butter in a large pot over medium heat. Add the onions and cook, stirring occasionally until soft, about 5 minutes. Add the garlic and cook, stirring occasionally, until fragrant, about 2 minutes. Add tomatoes and their juice to the pot, breaking apart tomatoes with your hands or the back of a wooden spoon. Add stock, red pepper, sugar, salt and ½ teaspoon of black pepper. Bring the soup to a boil, reduce heat to a simmer and cook for 20 minutes.

Remove from heat and carefully pour the soup mixture into a Vitamix or high-powered blender and blend until smooth, taking care when blending hot liquids. Return to a clean pot, taste and adjust seasonings. Add cream if using.

# CHICKEN TORTELLINI SOUP

Serves 6-8

In 2010, my husband was in a bike accident. After spending ten days in the hospital, we finally returned home to our three children, all under the age of six. During this challenging time, my sister-in-law came to our rescue by organizing a food chain. This chicken tortellini soup, made by my dear college friend's husband, was definitely one of our most memorable meals. A few weeks later, I reached out to him for the recipe, and here is my attempt at deciphering his casual "dude directions". This soup is both indulgent and comforting, yet still manages to be healthy. If you prefer a gluten-free option, you can easily substitute the tortellini with gluten-free pasta or rice, which is equally delicious. Every time I make this soup, it brings me back to that chaotic period, reminding me how fortunate I am to have Joey by my side, fully recovered, and even sporting some cool scars.

2 tablespoons olive oil
2 yellow onions, chopped
4 garlic cloves, minced
4 carrots, peeled and chopped
4 celery stalks, chopped
½ teaspoon dried oregano
½ teaspoon dried thyme
1 teaspoon salt
Freshly ground black pepper
8 cups chicken stock
2 whole roasted or rotisserie chickens
½ cup freshly grated parmesan or
   pecorino cheese plus more for topping
4 cups baby spinach
1 package of cheese tortellini

Heat the olive oil in a large soup pot over medium-high heat. Add the onions, garlic, carrots, celery, oregano, and thyme. Season with the salt and ¼ teaspoon of pepper and sauté until soft, about 10 minutes. Add the stock, bring to a boil, reduce the heat to a simmer and cook for 20 minutes.
Remove from heat and carefully pour the soup mixture into a Vitamix or high-powered blender and blend until smooth, taking care when blending hot liquids. Return the soup to a clean pot and add water or stock if the broth is too thick. Taste and adjust seasonings.

Pull the chicken meat off the bones, discard (or save the bones for making homemade stock). Shred the chicken and stir into the puréed soup. Bring to a boil, reduce to a simmer and cook on low for an hour. Once done, stir in the ½ cup cheese and spinach and remove from heat.

Meanwhile, cook tortellini according to package directions, and drain. When ready to serve, put a big spoonful of tortellini in a large bowl. Ladle warm soup over and top with freshly grated parmesan or pecorino cheese.

# WHITE BEAN, SAUSAGE & KALE SOUP

Serves 6-8

This hearty and nutritious soup is perfect for warming up on a chilly winter day. An added bonus is that it can be prepared in just 40 minutes and is gluten-free. Personally, I prefer using a combination of ground turkey and Italian sausage to make it slightly lighter, but you are welcome to use only sausage if you prefer.

2 tablespoons olive oil

1 medium yellow onion, diced

2 large carrots, peeled and diced

2 celery ribs, diced

½ pound ground turkey

½ pound mild Italian sausage
    (pork, turkey, or chicken), casings
    removed if using links

3 garlic cloves, minced

1 tablespoon tomato paste

¼ teaspoon red pepper flakes,
    plus more to taste

1 teaspoon salt, plus more to taste

4 cups chicken stock

2 (15-ounce) cans cannellini beans, drained
    and rinsed, or 1 ½ cups dried beans,
    soaked and cooked

1 bunch kale, center ribs removed

Heat the olive oil in a large soup pot over medium-high. Add the onion, carrots, and celery, and sauté until soft, about 6 minutes. Add the turkey and sausage and cook, breaking up the meat with your spoon, until the turkey is no longer pink, about 6 minutes. Add the garlic, tomato paste, red pepper flakes, and 1 teaspoon salt, and sauté for two more minutes. Add the stock and beans, bring to a boil then reduce to a simmer. Let simmer until the soup is thick, about 20 minutes.

Meanwhile roughly chop the kale leaves and add them to the pot and simmer until they are soft. Taste and adjust seasonings and serve in bowls topped with a drizzle of olive oil, freshly grated parmesan cheese and more red pepper flakes, if desired.

*Optional*

Top with olive oil
and freshly grated
parmesan
...................

# TUSCAN FARRO SOUP

Serves 6-8

Tuscan farro soup is a classic Italian soup, known for its comforting blend of vegetables and farro. Farro, a staple in Italian cuisine, is an ancient wheat variety. It boasts a delightful nutty flavor and is packed with fiber, protein, and various minerals and vitamins. It's important to note that farro does contain gluten, but it can be easily substituted with brown rice for a gluten-free option.

2 tablespoons olive oil

1 medium yellow onion, diced

2 large carrots, peeled and diced

2 celery ribs, diced

3 garlic cloves, minced

6 cups vegetable or chicken stock

1 (15-ounce) can diced tomatoes with juices

1 (15-ounce) white beans, drained and rinsed

1 cup pearled farro, rinsed

1 teaspoon salt

Freshly ground black pepper

1 Parmesan rind, optional

2 cups packed fresh baby spinach

¼ cup chopped parsley

1 teaspoon lemon juice or red wine vinegar

Heat the olive oil in a large soup pot over medium-high. Add the onion, carrots, celery and sauté until soft, about 5 minutes. Stir in the garlic and cook for another 2 minutes. Add stock, tomatoes, beans, farro, salt, pepper, and ¼ teaspoon of black pepper, parmesan rind (if using) and bring to a boil. Reduce to a simmer and cook, uncovered, until the farro is tender, about 30 minutes.

Turn the heat off and remove the parmesan rind. Stir in the spinach, parsley, and lemon juice or red wine vinegar. Ladle into large bowls and garnish with a drizzle of olive oil and freshly grated parmesan, if desired.

## *Optional*

Top with olive oil and freshly grated parmesan

..................

# MEXICAN

# SLOW COOKER WHITE BEAN CHILI

Serves 6-8

This white bean chicken chili will leave you satisfied and fulfilled without consuming too much of your valuable time. It is delicious, flavorful and requires minimal preparation. To make it even easier, it can be made in the slow cooker. Simply throw everything in, set it to cook on low all day, and by dinnertime, it is ready to enjoy!

2 tablespoons olive oil

1 medium yellow onion, chopped

2 garlic cloves, minced

1 (4-ounce) can diced green chilies, mild or hot

2 cups chicken stock

1 teaspoon ground cumin

1 teaspoon chili powder

½ teaspoon dried oregano

1 teaspoon salt

Freshly ground black pepper

1 ½ pounds boneless, skinless chicken breasts or thighs

2 (15-ounce) cans white beans (great northern, cannellini), drained and rinsed, or 1 ½ cups dried beans, cooked and drained

½ cup chopped cilantro

Juice of 1 lime

Heat the olive oil in a large skillet over medium heat. Add the onions and cook until soft, about 5 minutes. Add the garlic and cook until fragrant, about 2 minutes. Add green chilis, chicken stock, cumin, chili powder, oregano, salt and ¼ teaspoon of black pepper. Bring mixture to a boil then reduce to a simmer and cook for another 2 minutes.

Place the chicken in the bottom of a slow cooker and pour the onion broth over the chicken. Cover and cook on high for 4 hours or on low for 6 hours. When there is one hour left of cooking, remove the chicken, let it cool, shred it and add back to the slow cooker. Add beans and cook for another 1 hour.

Right before serving, stir in cilantro, lime juice and season with salt and pepper to taste. Ladle into big bowls and serve with optional toppings.

❋

*Optional*

Top with sour cream, grated jack cheese, red onions, cilantro, avocado

..................

# CHICKEN POZOLE VERDE

## Serves 6-8

Pozole is a traditional Mexican soup or stew that is deeply rooted in Mexican culture. It is a hearty and flavorful dish that typically includes hominy (lime-soaked corn kernels), meat, peppers and seasonings. There are various types of pozole, including red, white, and green. This green pozole (Pozole Verde) is usually made with chicken, tomatillos, and milder, tangy green chilies, like poblanos. Pozole is typically served with a variety of toppings, including shredded cabbage, diced onion, radish and lime.

6 cups chicken stock

2 pounds bone-in, skinless chicken breasts

2 bay leaves

1 onion, quartered

8 garlic cloves, peeled, divided

1 teaspoon salt

Freshly ground black pepper

1 pound tomatillos (about 12), husks removed, rinsed, and cut in half

2 poblano peppers, cut in half lengthwise, seeded and stemmed

1 to 2 jalapeño peppers (remove seeds for less heat)

1 tablespoon olive oil

½ yellow onion, roughly chopped

3 (15-ounce) cans white hominy, drained and rinsed

1 tablespoon oregano (preferably Mexican oregano)

1 teaspoon ground cumin

½ cup loosely packed fresh cilantro leaves

Preheat the oven to 450 degrees. Line a large baking sheet with foil and set aside.

Place the chicken stock, chicken breasts, bay leaves, onion, 6 of the garlic cloves, 1 teaspoon salt, and ¼ teaspoon of black pepper in a large soup pot. Bring to a boil then reduce heat to a simmer, cover, and cook until chicken is cooked through, about 20 minutes. Using a slotted spoon, transfer the chicken to a plate and discard the onion, garlic, and bay leaves. Once cool enough to handle, shred the chicken meat and return the chicken back to the stock.

Meanwhile, place the tomatillos, poblanos, and jalapenos on the prepared baking sheet. Drizzle with the olive oil and a large pinch of salt, toss, and arrange cut side down in an even layer. Roast, tossing a couple of times, until the tomatillos are soft and slightly browned, about 15 minutes.

*(recipe continues on page 67)*

❋

*Optional*

Top with shredded green cabbage, diced onion, minced cilantro, matchstick cut radishes, lime wedges, avocado, cotija

...................

Once the tomatillos and peppers are done, transfer them to a blender or food processor. Add 1 cup of the simmering broth, chopped onion, remaining 2 cloves of garlic, and cilantro, then blend until smooth. Add the blended sauce to the pot with the broth and chicken. Add hominy, oregano, cumin, and season with additional salt and pepper, to taste. Simmer for 15 more minutes. Ladle into big bowls and serve with the cilantro and optional toppings.

*Pro Tip!*

Canned hominy can be found in most grocery stores in the canned bean section. You can also make your own hominy by buying dry kernels. Treat them like you would dried beans, and rinse and soak them in water for several hours (or up to overnight) before simmering on low heat until tender.

...................

# PORK POZOLE ROJO

Serves 6-8

Red pozole (Pozole Rojo) is typically prepared with pork and a spicy red sauce made from dried chili peppers, such as guajillos and anchos. While green pozole has a tangy and slightly spicy flavor, red pozole has a smoky, robust flavor.

2 ounces dried guajillo chilis

2 ounces dried ancho chilis

2 pounds boneless pork shoulder, cut into 1 ½-inch cubes

Salt and pepper

1 tablespoon olive oil

1 medium yellow onion, diced

6 garlic cloves, minced, divided

6 cups chicken stock

3 (15-ounce) cans white hominy, drained and rinsed

2 bay leaves

1 tablespoon dried oregano (preferably Mexican oregano)

1 teaspoon ground cumin

❋

*Optional*

Top with shredded green cabbage, diced onion, minced cilantro, matchstick cut radishes, lime wedges, avocado, cotija

...................

Cut off the stems from the chilis and shake out the seeds to discard. Heat a cast iron skillet over medium heat, add chilis, and warm for a couple of minutes until soft and fragrant. Transfer the chilis to a heat-safe bowl, cover them completely with boiling water, and let soak for 30 minutes.

While the chilis are soaking, season the pork well with salt and black pepper. Heat the oil in a large soup pot over medium-high. Working in batches, add the pork and sear until all sides are lightly browned. Transfer the pork to a plate and set aside. Add the onions to the soup pot and cook until soft, about 5 minutes. Add 4 cloves of garlic and cook until fragrant, for about 2 minutes. Add the chicken stock, hominy, bay leaves, oregano, cumin, ½ teaspoon salt, and seared pork (with juices) and lower heat.

Place the soaked chilis and 1 ½ cups of the soaking liquid in a blender. Add the 2 remaining cloves of garlic, ½ teaspoon salt and blend until smooth. Strain through a fine-mesh sieve into a bowl, pushing the sauce through with a rubber spatula. Discard the solids. Pour the pureed chili sauce into the pot and stir to combine.

*(recipe continues on page 70)*

Bring soup to a boil, then reduce to a low simmer, cover, and cook for 1 ½ to 2 hours, stirring occasionally, until the pork is tender and shreds easily.

Remove the bay leaves and transfer the pork to a plate. Use two forks to shred the meat. Return the pork to the soup and stir to combine. Taste and season the soup with additional salt and pepper if needed. Add more stock if the broth is too thick. Ladle into big bowls and serve with optional toppings.

# ORANGE OCTOBER
# CHICKEN TORTILLA SOUP

Serves 6-8

This chicken tortilla soup is hearty, warming and incredibly satisfying. It offers a perfect combination of flavors in one bowl: a slightly spicy broth, tender chicken, black beans, juicy tomatoes, creamy avocado, and irresistibly crunchy tortilla strips on top. My boys enjoy it too, especially since I put all the garnishes in small bowls, allowing them to serve themselves. You can find "chipotle peppers in adobo sauce" in the canned section of most supermarkets. These are jalapeño chilis that have been dried, smoked and packed in a flavorful sauce made from tangy tomatoes and spices. Scale back if you don't like it spicy.

**For the soup:**

1 dried ancho chili or sub 1 teaspoon
    ancho chili powder
2 tablespoons olive oil
1 yellow onion, roughly chopped
3 garlic cloves, roughly chopped
1 to 2 chipotle chilis in adobo (depending
    on spice preference) plus 2 teaspoons sauce
1 teaspoon chili powder
1 teaspoon cumin
½ teaspoon dried oregano
1 teaspoon salt
1½ pounds boneless, skinless chicken breasts
1 (14 ½-ounce) can diced tomatoes
4 cups chicken stock
1 (15-ounce) can black beans
Juice from ½ a lime

**For the crunchy tortilla strips:**

¼ cup olive oil, plus more if needed
8 (6-inch) corn tortillas, sliced into ⅛ inch
    strips

*Optional*

Top with avocado, cotija,
cilantro, lime wedges
. . . . . . . . . . . . . . . . . .

If using the dried ancho chili, place it in a heat-safe bowl and cover it completely with boiling water. Let the chili soak for 20 minutes. Once soft, use your hands or a paring knife to remove the stems and seeds (wear cooking gloves if you're sensitive to the heat). Roughly chop and set aside.

Meanwhile, heat the 2 tablespoons of olive oil in a large soup pot over medium. Add the onions and cook until soft, about 5 minutes. Add the garlic and cook until fragrant, about 2 minutes. Add the chipotle and sauce, chili powder, cumin, oregano, and salt, and cook for another two minutes. Add chicken, tomatoes, and their juices, stock, and soaked ancho pepper (or ancho chili powder) and bring to a boil. Reduce to a simmer and cook for 20 minutes.

*(recipe continues on page 74)*

While the soup is simmering, make your crunchy tortilla strips. Heat ¼ cup olive oil in a frying pan over medium-high heat. Cut the tortillas into thin strips and fry them in batches in the hot oil until crisp, turning once. Remove them from the pan and place them on a paper towel-lined plate and sprinkle them with salt. Repeat with remaining tortilla strips, adding more oil if needed. Set aside.

When the chicken is done, set aside using a slotted spoon. Carefully pour the broth into a Vitamix or high-powered blender and blend until smooth, taking care when blending hot liquids. Return the soup to a clean pot.

Shred the chicken with your hands or two forks and return it to the soup along with the beans and the lime juice. Taste and adjust seasonings and simmer for 10 minutes. Ladle the soup into bowls and top with tortilla strips and optional toppings.

*Pro Tip!*

Substitute 2 cups of shredded rotisserie chicken instead of cooking the chicken breast.

....................

# EASY BLACK BEAN SOUP

Serves 6

This simple black bean soup is delicious and healthy. If you have the time to make your own beans, it will greatly enhance the flavor and nutritional value of the soup.

2 tablespoons olive oil

2 large onions, finely chopped (about 2 cups)

2 celery ribs, diced

4 garlic cloves, minced

1 jalapeño, seeded and diced

2 teaspoons ground cumin

1 teaspoon salt

Pinch of cayenne or freshly ground pepper

2 cups chicken or vegetable stock

3 (15-ounce) cans black beans, drained
   and rinsed or 1 pound black beans, soaked
   and cooked, reserving cooking liquid

## *Optional*

Top with avocado, sour cream,
queso fresco, cilantro, red onion,
corn chips, lime wedges,
pumpkin seeds

...................

Heat 2 tablespoons of oil in a large soup pot over medium. Add onion, celery, garlic, and jalapeño and sauté, stirring frequently, until soft, about 5 to 7 minutes. Do not brown. Add cumin, salt, cayenne or pepper and stir to coat the vegetables. If using homemade beans, pour the reserved bean cooking liquid into a large measuring cup and add enough stock to make 2 cups. Add the stock and the beans and bring to a boil. Reduce to a simmer, cover and cook for 15 minutes. Remove from heat.

Place 3 cups of black bean mixture into a blender and run until smooth, taking care when blending hot liquids. Return pureed soup to pot and stir to mix well. Add stock if the soup is too thick. Taste and adjust seasonings and ladle into bowls and serve with optional toppings.

# ALBÓNDIGAS SOUP
# (MEXICAN MEATBALL SOUP)

Serves 6

Mexican meatball soup, also known as Albóndigas soup, consists of meatballs, vegetables, tomatoes, spices, and chicken stock. Albóndigas, the Spanish term for "small meatballs," are traditionally made using ground beef and rice. Occasionally, I also prepare them using ground turkey or pork.

## For the meatballs:

1 pound lean ground beef or ground turkey

½ cup raw white rice, preferably long-grain
   or basmati

1 egg

2 garlic cloves, minced

1 teaspoon ground cumin

1 teaspoon dried oregano

2 tablespoons finely chopped cilantro

1 teaspoon salt

½ teaspoon freshly ground black pepper

## For the soup:

2 tablespoons olive oil

1 yellow onion, diced

2 carrots, peeled and diced

1 Russet potato, peeled and cut into
   ½-inch pieces

1 zucchini chopped into ½-inch dice

1 teaspoon cumin

1 teaspoon chili powder

1 teaspoon oregano

1 teaspoon salt

Freshly ground pepper

6 cups beef or chicken stock

1 (15-ounce) can fire roasted tomatoes

1 (15-ounce) can of black beans,
   drained and rinsed

Kernels from 2 ears corn or 1 cup of frozen corn

Preheat the oven to 400 degrees. Line a baking sheet with parchment paper. Place the ground meat, rice, egg, garlic, cumin, oregano, cilantro, salt, and black pepper in a large bowl and mix gently until just combined. Do not overmix. Using wet hands, roll the mixture into 1-inch balls and place onto the prepared baking sheet. Bake for 20 minutes until cooked through and lightly browned. Set aside. Meanwhile, heat the oil in a large pot over medium-high. Add the onion and cook for 5 minutes, until soft and translucent. Add the carrots, potato, zucchini, cumin, chili powder, oregano, salt and ¼ teaspoon of black pepper and cook for 8 to 10 minutes, stirring often. Add the stock and tomatoes, bring to a boil then reduce heat to a simmer and cook for 10 minutes. Add the meatballs, black beans, and corn to the pot. Simmer for an additional 5 to 10 minutes or until the corn is tender.
Taste and adjust seasonings and ladle into bowls and serve with optional toppings.

*Optional*

Top with avocado, sour cream, shredded cheese, cilantro, red onion, corn chips, lime wedges

..................

# GAME DAY BLACK BEAN TURKEY CHILI

## Serves 6-8

Turkey chili is an excellent alternative to traditional beef chili because it has lower fat and calorie content without sacrificing flavor or nutrition. I typically prepare a large batch of this chili on game days to offer a healthier option. An added bonus is that chili freezes exceptionally well, so I recommend doubling the recipe and storing some for a future meal.

2 tablespoons olive oil

1 large yellow onion, diced

2 garlic cloves, minced

1 pound ground turkey

2 tablespoons chili powder

1 tablespoon ground cumin

1 tsp salt

1 (28-ounce) can diced or crushed tomatoes

2 (15-ounce) cans black beans, drained, rinsed or 1 ½ cup dried beans, soaked and cooked

1 cup chicken stock

1 cup frozen corn kernels, optional

Heat the oil in a large pot over medium heat. Add the onion and cook until soft and translucent, about 5 minutes. Add the garlic and cook until fragrant, about 2 minutes. Add the ground turkey and cook, breaking up the meat with a wooden spoon, until no longer pink, about 5 minutes. Add the spices and salt and stir to mix well. Add the tomatoes, beans and stock and bring to a boil.

Reduce to a simmer and cook over low heat, stirring occasionally, until thickened, about 45 minutes. Add corn, if using, and simmer for another 5 minutes. Taste and adjust seasonings. Ladle into big bowls and serve with optional toppings.

## *Optional*

Top with avocado, sour cream, shredded cheese, cilantro, red onion
. . . . . . . . . . . . . . . . . .

# QUINOA CHILI

Serves 6-8

I'm sure many of you may think that the words "quinoa" and "chili" don't belong together, or that vegan chili might sound a little too healthy. However, rest assured that this incredibly satisfying meatless quinoa chili is so creamy and delicious, it will leave you with no second thoughts. Quinoa, recognized as one of the healthiest foods worldwide, is naturally gluten-free and packed with essential vitamins and minerals. It is also one of the few plant-based foods that provide a complete protein. When combined with beans, vegetables, and spices in this chili, you get a guilt-free, protein-packed bowl of yumminess.

1 cup quinoa, rinsed
2 tablespoons olive oil
1 yellow onion, diced
3 garlic cloves, minced
1 red bell pepper, chopped
2 tablespoons chili powder
2 teaspoons ground cumin
½ teaspoon cayenne pepper
1 teaspoon salt
1 (15-ounce) can pinto beans, drained, rinsed
    or 3/4 cup dried beans, soaked and cooked
1 (15-ounce) can black beans, drained, rinsed
    or 3/4 cup dried beans, soaked and cooked
1 (15-ounce) can chopped tomatoes
1 (15-ounce) can tomato puree
1 cup frozen corn kernels
2 tablespoons chopped cilantro
Juice of ½ lime

Cook quinoa according to package instructions. Set aside.

Heat olive oil in a large pot over medium-high. Add the onion and cook until soft and translucent, about 5 minutes. Add the garlic and cook until fragrant, about 2 minutes. Add the bell pepper, chili powder, cumin, cayenne, and salt and stir to coat and cook for another 2 minutes.

Stir in cooked quinoa, beans, chopped tomatoes, and tomato sauce, and mix well. Bring to a boil. Reduce heat to low and simmer, covered, until thickened, about 30 minutes. Add water to thin if necessary. Stir in corn, cilantro, and lime juice, and cook for about 10 minutes. Ladle in big bowls and serve with optional toppings.

*Optional*

Top with avocado, sour cream, shredded cheese, cilantro, red onion
..................

# VEGETARIAN & VEGAN

# BUTTERNUT SQUASH, BROWN RICE & MUSHROOM SOUP

Serves 6-8

I tend to make this soup as soon as the kids go back to school after summer break. The combination of sweet squash, robust mushrooms, and nutty brown rice is absolutely delicious. It is a hearty and healthy dish that I could happily enjoy every fall day.

1 cup brown rice

2 tablespoons butter or olive oil

1 medium onion, diced

3 carrots, peeled and diced

3 celery stalks, diced

2 portobello mushrooms, cleaned, stemmed and cut into ½-inch pieces

2 cups butternut squash, peeled and cut into ½-inch cubes

1 teaspoon salt

Freshly ground black pepper

6 to 8 cups chicken or vegetable stock

1 bunch curly kale, center ribs removed and roughly chopped

Rinse brown rice well and cook according to package directions.

Meanwhile, heat butter or oil in a large heavy soup pot over medium heat. Add the onion and sauté until soft and translucent, about 6 minutes. Add the carrots and celery and cook for another 5 minutes. Add the mushrooms, squash, salt, and ¼ teaspoon of fresh black pepper and cook, stirring often for another 10 minutes. If the pot dries out, add a little water.

Add the stock, bring to a boil, reduce to a simmer and cook for 20 minutes. Add the kale, and cook for another 5 to 10 minutes. Turn the heat off and add the cooked brown rice. Taste and adjust seasonings.

✳

*Optional*

Top with freshly
grated parmesan

...................

# CORN SOUP

Serves 4-6

This corn soup is so incredibly rich and creamy that it is hard to believe it doesn't contain any cream. With just a small amount of butter, onions, corn, water, and one cup of milk, it is absolutely delicious. For garnish, I usually add some chopped fried bacon (omit if vegetarian), a dollop of creme fraîche, and a sprinkle of fresh basil leaves. To make it vegan, you can substitute the butter with olive oil, omit the milk, and only use basil as a topping. Serve it warm or at room temperature.

6 ears corn
2 tablespoons olive oil or butter
1 onion, chopped
1 teaspoon salt
Freshly ground black pepper
1 cup milk, optional

✳

*Optional*

Top with crumbled
bacon, fresh basil,
crème fraîche
...................

Shuck and clean corn well. Cut the kernels off each ear and set aside. Heat the olive oil or butter in a large soup pot over medium heat. Add the onion and cook until soft and translucent, about 5 minutes. Add the corn to the pot and enough water to just barely cover the corn. Bring to a boil, reduce to a simmer, and cook for 15 to 20 minutes.

Remove from the heat and carefully pour the mixture into a Vitamix or high-powered blender. Blend until smooth, taking care when blending hot liquids. Pour the blended soup into a strainer over a clean pot (use a wooden spoon to help push the soup through the strainer). Add the salt, ¼ teaspoon of fresh black pepper, and 1 cup of milk, if using. Ladle into bowls and serve with the optional bacon pieces and snipped fresh basil.

# CURRIED SWEET POTATO SOUP

*Serves 4-6*

This soup is one of my all-time favorite soups to make during the fall and winter seasons. The combination of sweet potatoes, warm spices, and coconut milk creates a delightful puree that is both comforting and flavorful. Not only is it incredibly easy to make, but it is also naturally vegan and gluten-free.

2 tablespoons coconut oil
1 yellow onion, roughly chopped
1 tablespoon freshly grated ginger
2 garlic cloves, minced
1 tablespoon curry powder
1 teaspoon ground cumin
1 teaspoon ground turmeric
1 teaspoon salt
Freshly ground black pepper
2 pounds sweet potatoes, peeled
   and cut into 1-inch pieces
3 to 4 cups vegetable stock
1 tablespoon of Sriracha, optional
1 (15-ounce) can coconut milk

Heat coconut oil in a large pot over medium heat. Add onions and sauté until soft and translucent, about 6 minutes. Add ginger and garlic and cook for 2 more minutes. Stir in the curry, cumin, turmeric, salt and ¼ teaspoon of fresh black pepper. Cook for another 2 minutes. Add the potatoes and stock and bring to a boil. Reduce heat to a simmer, cover, and cook for 15 to 20 minutes, or until the potato is soft.

Remove from the heat and carefully pour the mixture into a Vitamix or high-powered blender. Blend until smooth, taking care when blending hot liquids. Stir in the Sriracha, if using, and the coconut milk. Taste and adjust seasonings.

Ladle soup into bowls and serve with optional toppings.

\*

*Optional*
Top with yogurt,
cilantro, roasted
cashews
...................

# DETOX LENTIL & SPLIT PEA SOUP

Serves 6-8

Packed with vitamins, minerals, protein, and fiber, this soup is an ideal nutrient-rich detox soup. It can be effortlessly prepared in a crockpot or pressure cooker by transferring the sautéed veggies to the slow cooker, adding lentils, split peas, and stock, and cooking on high for 4 hours. It is gluten-free and vegan (if vegetable broth is used), but I personally enjoy mine with a sprinkle of grated parmesan.

2 tablespoons olive oil
1 medium onion, diced
2 garlic cloves, minced
3 carrots, peeled and diced
3 celery stalks, diced
2 cups butternut squash
   (peeled and cut into ½ inch cubes)
1 teaspoon salt
Freshly ground black pepper
1 cup green or brown lentils, picked
   over and rinsed
¾ cup yellow split peas (or just use
   more lentils), picked over and rinsed
8 to 10 cups vegetable or chicken stock
2 to 3 cups spinach or kale,
   center ribs removed, chopped
Juice of ½ lemon

Heat oil in a large soup pot over medium heat. Add onions and sauté until soft and translucent, about 6 minutes. Add garlic and cook for 2 more minutes. Add carrots, celery, squash, salt and ¼ teaspoon of fresh black pepper. Cook, stirring often, until vegetables are soft, about 10 minutes.

Add lentils, split peas, and stock, and bring to a boil, reduce to a simmer, partially cover and cook until legumes are soft, about 40 minutes.

Place about 3 cups of soup in a blender. Process until smooth and add back to the pot and stir to combine. Stir in the kale and simmer for five minutes. Turn the heat off, taste and adjust seasonings, and add lemon juice.

Serve in bowls with a sprinkle of grated parmesan, if desired.

✳

*Optional*

Top with freshly
grated parmesan
...................

# SUPER GREEN ALKALIZING SOUP

Serves 4-6

This is the ultimate salad, in soup form. Loaded with fresh alkaline vegetables that are rich in vitamins, minerals, and antioxidants, this nutritious green soup will reduce your body's acidity and nourish your cells. Additionally, it can be enjoyed cold as well.

2 tablespoons olive oil

1 onion, chopped

1 leek, white and light green parts, chopped

2 celery stems, roughly chopped

1 head broccoli, chopped into florets

4 garlic cloves, roughly chopped

1 teaspoon cumin powder

1 teaspoon salt

Freshly ground black pepper

2 cups vegetable stock

2 cups (tightly packed) kale leaves, roughly chopped

5 cups (tightly packed) baby spinach leaves

Zest and juice of one lemon

Heat olive oil in a large soup pot over medium heat. Add onions, leeks, celery, and broccoli and sauté until soft, about 6 minutes. Add garlic, cumin, salt and ¼ teaspoon of black pepper and cook for 2 more minutes. Add the broth, bring to a simmer and cook the vegetables, stirring occasionally for 10 minutes. Add the kale and spinach and cook until leaves wilt, about 2 minutes.

Remove the pot from the heat and carefully pour the mixture into a Vitamix or high-powered blender. Blend until smooth, taking care when blending hot liquids. Return to a clean pot, stir in lemon juice and zest. Taste and adjust seasonings.

# SPRING ASPARAGUS SOUP

Serves 6

I always prepare this soup around St. Patrick's Day because not only is it green, but mid-March also marks the beginning of spring and asparagus season. This creamy soup is incredibly simple to make and truly highlights the freshness of spring asparagus. Furthermore, it is naturally gluten-free, vegetarian, and can be made dairy-free by omitting the use of butter and crème fraîche.

2 tablespoons butter or olive oil

1 yellow onion, peeled and chopped

1 teaspoon minced garlic or 1
    tablespoon minced green garlic

2 bunches asparagus, woody ends snapped off

4 cups vegetable or chicken stock

½ teaspoon salt

Freshly ground black pepper

1 teaspoon lemon juice

½ cup heavy cream, optional

Heat butter or oil in a large soup pot over medium heat. Add onions and sauté until soft, about 6 minutes. Add garlic and cook for 2 more minutes. Slice the asparagus crosswise into ½-inch pieces and add them to the pot. Cook the vegetables for 10 minutes, stirring occasionally. Add the stock, salt, and ¼ teaspoon of fresh black pepper, then bring to a boil. Reduce heat to a simmer and cook for another 10 minutes.

Remove the pot from the heat and carefully pour the mixture into a Vitamix or high-powered blender. Blend until smooth, taking care when blending hot liquids. Return to a clean pot, stir in lemon juice and cream (if using). Taste and adjust seasonings.

Ladle soup into bowls and garnish with julienned basil and a dollop of crème fraîche.

✳

*Optional*
Top with julienned
basil, crème
fraîche
...................

# BUTTERNUT SQUASH SOUP

Serves 6

Butternut squash soup is a popular classic fall dish that is enjoyed by nearly everyone. I personally like to roast my butternut squash before preparing the soup for a deeper, richer flavor, but you can easily skip this step. Additionally, this soup is naturally gluten-free and vegan-friendly when vegetable stock is used.

1 (3-pound) butternut squash, peeled, seeded, and cut into 1-inch cubes

4 tablespoons olive oil, divided

1 teaspoon sea salt, divided

Freshly ground black pepper

1 yellow onion, peeled and roughly chopped

2 garlic cloves, chopped

4 cups chicken or vegetable stock

1 tablespoon maple syrup

✳

*Optional*
Top with fresh thyme,
toasted bread
....................

Preheat the oven to 400 degrees and line a baking sheet with parchment paper. Place the cubed squash on the baking sheet and drizzle with 2 tablespoons olive oil, ½ teaspoon salt and a few grinds of black pepper. Toss to combine. Spread the squash in an even layer and bake until squash is tender and golden at the edges, about 30 minutes, turning halfway.

Meanwhile, heat remaining 2 tablespoons of oil in a large soup pot over medium heat. Add onions and sauté until soft, about 6 minutes. Add garlic and cook for 2 more minutes. Add the roasted squash, stock, remaining ½ teaspoon of salt, and more black pepper, to taste. Bring to a boil. Reduce heat to a simmer and cook for 15 minutes.

Remove from the heat and carefully pour mixture into a Vitamix or high-powered blender. Blend until smooth, taking care when blending hot liquids. Return to a clean pot, stir in maple syrup. Taste and adjust seasonings and garnish with optional toppings.

# SPRING GREEN MINESTRONE WITH PESTO

Serves 6

Spring is actually one of my favorite seasons for enjoying soup. Even though the sun is shining and temperatures rise, there is still a subtle chill in the air that makes me crave a comforting bowl of warmth. And, when it comes to spring soups, there is nothing quite like this heavenly green minestrone. It is light and bursting with the flavors of crisp, green Spring vegetables. If you opt for store-bought pesto, ensure it is of high quality. The only caution to keep in mind is that this soup does not store well as the vegetables tend to become soggy.

2 tablespoons olive oil

1 small onion, diced

2 small leeks, cut in half lengthwise, cleaned and chopped into ½-inch pieces

2 green garlic stalks, white and light green parts, or 2 large garlic cloves, minced

1 bunch asparagus, tips removed, ends trimmed, and cut on the diagonal into 1-inch pieces

1 teaspoon salt

Freshly ground black pepper

4 cups vegetable or chicken stock

1 (15-ounce) can cannellini beans, drained and rinsed

1 cup fresh or frozen peas

2 cups baby spinach leaves

Heat olive oil in a large soup pot over medium heat. Add the onions and leeks and sauté until soft, about 6 minutes. Add the garlic and cook for 2 more minutes, until fragrant. Add the asparagus, salt, and ¼ teaspoon of fresh black pepper and stir to mix well. Add the chicken stock and cannellini beans, bring to a boil, reduce the heat and cook for about five minutes. Add the peas and cook for another two minutes.

Remove from heat, stir in spinach leaves. Taste and adjust seasonings. Serve with fresh pesto and/or grated parmesan.

✳

*Optional*
Top with fresh or high-quality store-bought pesto, parmesan cheese
··················

# GREEN OR RED LENTIL CURRY

Serves 6

Lentils and curry pair perfectly in this delightful vegetarian stew, sure to become one of your weekly staples. Bursting with flavor and incredibly easy to make, this dish features simmered lentils and vegetables in a well-seasoned coconut milk broth that offers a rich earthiness and comforting warmth. Serve this hearty stew over a bed of warm rice, and add a garnish of cilantro and plain yogurt for a finishing touch.

2 tablespoons olive or coconut oil

1 yellow onion, minced

1 tablespoon ginger, peeled and grated

4 garlic cloves, minced

1 ½ tablespoons curry powder

1 teaspoon ground turmeric

1 teaspoon ground cumin

1 teaspoon salt

Freshly ground black pepper

2 medium carrots, peeled and diced

1 small butternut squash or sweet potato, peeled and cut into 1-inch pieces

1 cup red or green lentils, rinsed

3 cups vegetable or chicken stock

1 (15-ounce) can coconut milk

Heat the oil in a large saucepan over medium-high heat. Add the onion and cook until soft and translucent, about 6 minutes. Add the ginger and garlic and cook, stirring frequently, for another minute. Stir in the curry powder, turmeric, cumin, salt, ¼ teaspoon of fresh black pepper, carrots, butternut squash, and lentils, and stir to coat. Add the stock and the coconut milk and bring to a boil. Reduce the heat to a simmer and cook, stirring occasionally, until lentils and vegetables are tender, about 20 minutes.

Ladle into big bowls and serve with optional toppings. Also delicious over white rice.

✳

*Optional*
Top with cilantro and yogurt
and serve with naan
and steamed rice
..................

# PEA SOUP

Serves 4-6

Whether served hot or cold, this delightful soup can be enjoyed as a flavorful appetizer or a satisfying lunch, whether served hot or cold. Its vibrant green hue, velvety consistency, and subtle taste truly make it a special treat. For an extra touch, garnish with a dollop of crème fraîche and a sprinkle of fresh chives.

2 tablespoons butter or olive oil
1 onion, roughly chopped
4 cups shelled fresh or frozen peas
    (defrosted in a sieve under warm
    running water)
2 cups chicken or vegetable stock
¼ cup chopped mint
1 teaspoon salt
Freshly ground pepper
¼ cup heavy cream

Heat the butter or olive oil in a large saucepan, add the onion, and cook over medium heat for 5 to 10 minutes, until the onion is tender. Add the peas and broth. Bring to a boil, then reduce the heat to medium-low and cook, uncovered, for 5 minutes. Off the heat, add the mint, salt, and ¼ teaspoon of fresh black pepper.

Carefully pour the mixture into a Vitamix or high-powered blender. Blend until smooth, taking care when blending hot liquids. Add water to thin if necessary.

Pour into a clean pot, taste and adjust seasonings, and serve with the optional chives and crème fraîche.

✳

*Optional*
Top with chives and
crème fraîche
....................

# CARROT SOUP

Serves 4-6

This incredibly easy carrot soup, made with only four ingredients, is not only beautiful and healthy but also gluten-free and vegetarian. Ready in under 30 minutes, this soup is packed with an abundance of beta-carotene that may enhance your vision. If you enjoy carrot/ginger soup, feel free to add some chopped ginger. Additionally, you can substitute butter with oil to make it vegan-friendly.

2 tablespoons butter or olive oil
2 large shallots, chopped, yielding about 1 cup
1 ½ pounds carrots, peeled and chopped
   (6 to 8 large carrots)
2 teaspoons fresh ginger, grated (optional)
½ teaspoon salt
Freshly ground black pepper
2 to 3 cups chicken or vegetable stock

Melt olive oil or butter in a medium soup pot over medium heat. Add shallots and cook until soft, about 5 minutes. Add carrots, ginger if using, salt and ¼ teaspoon of fresh black pepper and stir to coat. Add enough stock to just barely cover the carrots. Bring to a boil, reduce heat to a simmer, cover and cook until carrots are soft, about 15 minutes.

Remove from heat and transfer to a blender and puree until smooth, remembering to take caution when blending hot liquids. Transfer to a clean pot and add water if necessary to thin soup. Taste and adjust seasonings and serve with freshly snipped chives and coconut milk.

*

*Optional*
Top with fresh chives,
coconut milk
...................

# ZUCCHINI, CAULIFLOWER & LEEK SOUP

Serves 4-6

This creamy vegetarian soup is an easy and guaranteed crowd-pleaser . With just five simple ingredients and 20 minutes of cooking time, you can enjoy a healthy and delicious soup. Enjoy it on its own or garnish with crème fraîche and parsley.

2 tablespoons butter or olive oil
2 medium leeks, white and light-green parts, cut in half lengthwise, thinly sliced and cleaned
4 zucchinis, chopped into 1-inch pieces
1 small head cauliflower, cored and chopped into florets
4 cups vegetable or chicken stock
1 teaspoon salt
Freshly ground black pepper

Heat butter or olive oil in a large soup pot over medium heat. Add the leeks and sauté until soft, about 5 minutes. Add the zucchini and cauliflower and cook for another 10 minutes, stirring often. Add stock and bring to a boil. Reduce to a simmer and cook for 15 to 20 minutes.

Remove from the heat and carefully pour the mixture into a Vitamix or high-powered blender. Blend until smooth, taking care when blending hot liquids. Add water to thin if necessary.

Pour into a clean pot, add the salt and ¼ teaspoon of fresh black pepper, taste, adjust seasonings, and serve with the optional parsley and crème fraîche.

✳

*Optional*
Top with parsley and
crème fraîche
..................

# CHICKPEA & KALE STEW

Serves 6

This chickpea and kale stew exemplifies the beauty of simplicity in food. It serves as a perfect side dish and pairs well with almost any main course. With just seven simple ingredients and around 30 minutes of preparation time, it is quick and easy to make.

2 tablespoons olive oil
1 yellow onion, chopped
2 garlic cloves, minced
2 tablespoons chopped parsley
½ teaspoon salt
¼ teaspoon dried chili flakes
1 (15-ounce) can crushed tomatoes
1 cup chicken or vegetable stock,
    plus extra for thinning if needed
2 (15-ounce) cans chickpeas,
    drained and rinsed
2 cups roughly chopped curly kale leaves
Freshly grated parmesan

Heat olive oil in a large pot over medium heat. Add the onion and cook until soft and translucent, about 6 minutes. Add the garlic and sauté for another 2 minutes. Add the parsley, salt, and chili flakes and stir well. Add the tomatoes, stock, and chickpeas, and bring to a boil. Reduce heat to a simmer and cook, stirring occasionally, for 20 to 30 minutes.

Add the chopped kale and cook for another 10 minutes.

Taste and adjust seasonings, and serve with grated parmesan.

✳

*Optional*
Top with freshly
shaved parmesan
. . . . . . . . . . . . . . . . . . .

# ROASTED CAULIFLOWER SOUP WITH GRILLED CHEESE CROUTONS

Serves 4-6

The secret to getting kids to enjoy soup is adding these tasty croutons. They're easy to make and add a delicious touch to every spoonful of soup. The bread soaks up the soup so even if the kids only eat the croutons, they'll still be getting some of the purée. This roasted cauliflower soup is a staple in our house, made with just six simple ingredients. It's nourishing, silky, and absolutely delicious. Plus, it's vegetarian, gluten-free (substitute GF bread), healthy, and light.

1 large head cauliflower (about 2 ½ pounds), chopped into florets
4 tablespoons olive oil
½ teaspoon salt
1 onion, chopped
2 garlic cloves, minced
4 cups chicken or vegetable stock
4 pieces sourdough bread
4 pieces sharp cheddar cheese
Softened butter, for smearing on bread

Preheat the oven to 400 degrees. Line a baking sheet with parchment paper. Place cauliflower on the baking sheet and toss with 2 tablespoons olive oil and salt and spread in a single layer. Roast cauliflower until golden brown, about 20 minutes.

Meanwhile, heat remaining 2 tablespoons of olive oil (or butter) in a large soup pot over medium heat. Add the onions and sauté until soft and translucent, about 6 minutes. Add the garlic and cook for 2 more minutes, until fragrant. Add the roasted cauliflower and stock and bring to a boil. Reduce the heat and simmer for 10 minutes.

Remove from the heat and transfer to a blender and puree until smooth, remembering to take caution when blending hot liquids. Transfer the soup to a clean pot and add water if necessary to thin the soup. Taste and adjust seasonings.

For the grilled cheese croutons: put two pieces of cheese between two slices of sourdough bread and butter on the outside of each. Grill in a cast iron skillet or a panini machine, until golden brown and cheese melted. Put on a cutting board to cool. Remove crusts and cut sandwiches into ½-inch square croutons.

Ladle soup into bowls and top with croutons.

# ASIAN INSPIRED

# CHICKEN RAMEN

## Serves 4

My boys have a deep love for top ramen. It's their favorite after-school snack. While I appreciate their independence in cooking for themselves, I am not a fan of the additives and preservatives found in packaged ramen. That's why I decided to start making my own. This homemade chicken ramen recipe is bursting with incredible flavors and still simple enough to whip up for dinner. The combination of ramen noodles in a rich, savory shoyu (soy sauce) broth, topped with succulent soy-marinated chicken and a kick of chili garlic oil, surpasses anything you can find in a package. Even the boys are in complete agreement!

**For the chicken marinade:**
1 to 2 tablespoons sriracha
2 tablespoons brown sugar or honey
2 tablespoons soy sauce
1 tablespoon mirin
1 teaspoon sesame oil
2 garlic cloves, minced
1 ½ pounds boneless chicken thighs, skin on or off depending on preference

**For the soup:**
4 cups chicken stock
¼ cup soy sauce
2 tablespoons mirin
4 scallions, trimmed and cut in half lengthwise
2-inch piece of ginger, peeled and cut into 6 coin sized rounds
3 garlic cloves, crushed
1 teaspoon black peppercorns
1 cup sliced shiitake mushrooms
3 heads baby bok choy, trimmed, cleaned and cut into thirds
4 eggs
2 (3-ounce) packages of ramen noodles

**For the chili garlic oil:**
1 tablespoon sesame oil
¼ cup avocado oil or vegetable oil
3 garlic cloves, minced
2 tablespoons crushed red chili flakes
1 tablespoon toasted sesame seeds

**For the chicken:**
Place all the ingredients for the chicken marinade in a bowl and mix well. Add the chicken and stir to coat. Allow chicken to marinate for at least 1 hour and up to 12 hours.

Preheat the oven to 425 degrees and line a baking sheet with parchment paper. Place the marinated chicken on the baking sheet and roast until the chicken is cooked, about 25 minutes.

**For the soup:**
While the chicken is cooking, make the soup. Place chicken stock, soy sauce, mirin, scallions, ginger, garlic, and peppercorns in a large soup pot over medium heat. Bring mixture to a boil, cover, reduce heat to low, and simmer the soup for 30 minutes. Using a slotted spoon, remove the scallions, garlic, ginger, and peppercorns from the broth. Add the mushrooms and bok choy and simmer for another 5 minutes.

*(recipe continues page 121)*

Meanwhile, bring a medium pot of water to a boil and in a medium-sized bowl, prepare an ice water bath. Lower heat to a rapid simmer and using a slotted spoon, carefully lower the eggs into the water and let simmer for 4 minutes. Remove the eggs with a slotted spoon and place the eggs in the ice water. Once cool enough to handle, peel the eggs, cut them in half lengthwise and set aside.

Return the pot of water to a boil and cook ramen noodles according to package directions, discarding any flavor packets. Drain the noodles and divide them evenly among four bowls. Ladle the hot soup over the noodles and top with the sliced chicken, eggs, and sesame seeds.

**For the chili garlic oil:**
Heat oils in a small saucepan over medium heat. Once hot, add the garlic and fry, stirring often until garlic is fragrant, about 2 minutes, taking care not to burn the garlic. Stir in red chilis, sesame seeds, sugar, and salt, and cook for an additional minute. Mix well and allow to cool. Store in a glass airtight container in the fridge for up to a month.

# WONTON SOUP

Serves 6

You might find it hard to believe, but making wontons is actually pretty easy. The best part is, they freeze exceptionally well too. Whenever I prepare them, I always make a double batch and freeze half, ensuring that I can whip up a delicious soup whenever I need it. To freeze the wontons, simply arrange them on a plate lined with parchment paper, loosely cover them with plastic wrap, and let them freeze completely, which usually takes about 2 hours. Afterward, transfer them to a plastic bag. The great thing is that you can cook them straight from frozen, just remember to add an extra 1 to 2 minutes to the cooking time.

**For the wonton filling:**

½ pound of ground pork

½ cup finely shredded green cabbage

2 green onions, finely chopped

1 tablespoon soy sauce

1 teaspoon sesame oil

1 teaspoon fresh ginger, grated

1 garlic clove, minced

24 square 3 ½-inch wonton wrappers

**For the broth:**

6 cups chicken stock

2 garlic cloves, crushed

1-inch piece of ginger, peeled and
    cut into 3 coin-sized rounds

2 tablespoons soy sauce

1 teaspoon sesame oil

2 green onions, white and
    light green parts, thinly sliced

**For the wontons:**

Combine all the filling ingredients in a large bowl. Line a baking sheet with parchment paper. Place 1 heaping teaspoon of filling into the center of each wonton wrapper. Moisten the edges with a little water and fold in half to create a triangle. Moisten the two longer tips and bring them together and seal. It should look like a big tortellini. Place the wontons on the prepared baking sheet. Repeat with remaining wrappers.

**For the broth:**

In a medium-sized pot over medium heat add chicken broth, garlic, ginger, soy sauce, sesame oil, and green onions and bring to a boil. Reduce to a simmer for 10 minutes. Remove the garlic and ginger using a slotted spoon and discard. Bring a separate large pot of water to boil. Place wontons in water and cook for 4 minutes or until they float. Remove with a slotted spoon straight into serving bowls. Ladle broth over the wontons.

# PHO

Serves 4

Pho, pronounced as f-ah, is an authentic Vietnamese noodle soup consisting of an aromatic garlic-ginger infused broth, rice noodles, and various toppings such as thinly sliced beef or chicken, fresh herbs, lime, chilies, and bean sprouts. While the traditional pho soup usually demands hours of preparation, I have discovered a quick version that is equally delicious. In less than an hour, you can enjoy this incredibly satisfying and nurturing dish. This recipe features beef, but don't hesitate to substitute it with shredded rotisserie chicken if you prefer.

4 whole star anise

3 whole cloves

1 cinnamon stick

1 teaspoon black peppercorns

1 tsp coriander seed

8 cups beef stock

1 tablespoon brown sugar (optional)

2-inch piece fresh ginger, peeled and cut into 6 coin sized rounds

1 tablespoon fish sauce

1 yellow onion, peeled and cut into quarters

½ teaspoon salt

1 pound beef sirloin, thinly sliced

6 ounces rice noodles

❋

*Optional*

Garnish with bean sprouts, basil leaves, mint leaves, cilantro leaves, chopped green onions, Thai chili or serrano, thinly sliced, lime wedges

..................

To make the broth, place a large soup pot over medium-high heat, add the star anise, cloves, cinnamon, peppercorns, and coriander seeds, and toast, stirring often, until fragrant, about 1 minute. Add the stock, sugar, fish sauce, ginger, and onion. Bring to a boil, reduce the heat, and simmer for 20-30 minutes.

While the broth is cooking, cover the beef with plastic wrap and place it in the freezer for 15 minutes to make it easier to slice. Remove the beef from the freezer and slice the beef across the grain into very thin slices, about ¼-inch thick. Cover and put in the fridge until ready to serve.

When the broth is done, pour it through a fine mesh strainer into a clean pot, discarding the solids. Taste and adjust seasonings and keep the broth warm over low heat.

Prepare the rice noodles according to the package directions. Drain the noodles, then run them under cool water to stop cooking. Divide the noodles among four bowls and top with a few sirloin slices. Bring the broth to a boil and then pour the hot broth into the bowls, making sure to submerge the meat completely so that it gets cooked.

Top with bean sprouts, herbs, green onions, chili, and lime.

# ASIAN CHICKEN NOODLE

Serves 6

Part pho, part Chinese egg drop soup, this soup has all those yummy Asian flavors that truly warm the heart and the soul. Loaded with vegetables and health-boosting aromatics (garlic and ginger), it happens to be the perfect remedy for any sickness.

2 tablespoons vegetable oil

2 leeks, trimmed, halved lengthwise, cleaned, and cut into ½-inch slices

3 carrots, peeled and cut into ½-inch pieces

3 celery stalks, cut into ½-inch slices

2 garlic cloves, minced

2-inch piece of ginger, peeled and grated

½ bunch of cilantro, tied together, plus leaves for garnish

6 cups chicken stock

½ cup mirin

2 tablespoons tamari or soy sauce

1 teaspoon sea salt

1 teaspoon red pepper flakes

Zest and juice from 1 lime

2 pounds boneless, skinless chicken breasts

3 heads baby bok choy, trimmed and quartered widthwise

8 radishes, cut into eighths

6 ounces Asian noodles (egg or rice)

Heat the vegetable oil in a large soup pot over medium-high heat. Add the leeks, carrots, and celery and cook, stirring often until soft, about 5 minutes. Add the garlic and ginger and cook for another 2 minutes. Add the tied cilantro and stir to combine.

Pour in the stock, mirin, tamari or soy sauce, sea salt, pepper flakes, lime zest and juice from half of the lime. Add the chicken pieces, bring to a boil, turn heat to low, cover and cook for 30 minutes. When done, remove the chicken and let the soup simmer uncovered.

Once cooled, shred the chicken with your hands or two forks and return it to the soup. Add the remaining lime juice and lime zest, bok choy and radishes and cook for another 5 minutes. Remove the cilantro and discard. Taste and adjust seasonings.

When ready to serve, cook noodles according to package directions, drain and divide noodles evenly among soup bowls. Ladle the soup into each bowl and top with a drop of chili oil, cilantro leaves, and sriracha if desired.

*Optional*

Garnish with ½ teaspoon chili oil (recipe on page 118), cilantro leaves, sriracha

..................

# THAI SHRIMP COCONUT SOUP

Serves 4

Reminiscent of Laksa, a classic Malaysian spicy coconut curry noodle soup featuring shrimp, this mouthwatering soup is incredibly simple to prepare. All you need to do is blend a fragrant spice paste in a food processor, gently simmer it in creamy coconut milk, and add fresh shrimp. In just twenty minutes, it will taste as though you dedicated several hours in the kitchen. Adjust the spiciness according to your preference by adjusting the amount of chili peppers.

**For the red curry paste:**

2 shallots, peeled and roughly chopped

4 garlic cloves

2 tablespoons red chili paste

1 to 2 red chilis, fresh (optional)

2 stalks lemongrass, outer layer removed, white part only, roughly chopped

1 teaspoon ground turmeric

½ teaspoon salt

**For the broth:**

1 (15-ounce) can coconut milk

2 cups chicken stock

3 tablespoons lime juice

2 tablespoons fish sauce

2 teaspoons brown sugar

1 pound rice noodles of your choice

1 pound shrimp, peeled and deveined, tails removed, if desired

Put all ingredients for the paste in a food processor and run until smooth, scraping down the sides a couple of times.

Heat a large soup pot and add the paste and a little bit of coconut milk, about 3 tablespoons. Let simmer for 3 to 4 minutes then add the rest of the coconut milk, chicken broth, lime juice, fish sauce, and sugar and simmer for 15 minutes.

Meanwhile, cook noodles according to the package directions as set aside. Add the shrimp to the soup pot and simmer for 3 to 4 minutes until cooked. Remove from the heat, taste and adjust seasonings. To serve, divide the noodles between 4 large, shallow bowls and ladle the shrimp and broth over each.

Garnish with cilantro, basil, sprouts, and lime, and serve immediately.

*Optional*

Top with cilantro leaves, basil leaves, sprouts, lime wedges

..................

# CHICKEN CONGEE

Serves 4-6

Congee, also referred to as porridge, is a renowned breakfast delicacy that is popular across various regions in Asia. This comforting dish consists of tender chicken and creamy rice cooked in a delightful garlic-ginger infused broth. Its flavors are rich and satisfying, making it a perfect choice to start your day.

**For the congee:**
2 tablespoons vegetable oil
2 medium shallots, diced
1 tablespoon minced peeled ginger
1 tablespoon minced garlic
6 cups chicken stock
2 tablespoons fish sauce
1 teaspoon sugar
1 pound boneless, skinless chicken thighs
    or breasts
½ teaspoon salt
Freshly ground black pepper
1 cup uncooked jasmine rice

**For the fried shallots:**
¼ avocado or grapeseed oil
2 large shallots, peeled and thinly sliced

*Optional*
Top with chili oil, chopped cilantro, scallions, soft-boiled egg, lime slices
. . . . . . . . . . . . . . . . .

Heat the vegetable oil in a large soup pot over medium heat. Add the shallots, ginger, and garlic and cook, stirring often, until fragrant, about 2 minutes. Add the stock, fish sauce, sugar, chicken, salt, and a few grinds of fresh black pepper, and bring to a boil. Reduce to a simmer and cook uncovered, for 20 minutes, or until meat is cooked through. Remove chicken with tongs and set aside to cool. Once cool, chop or shred into bite sized pieces.

Meanwhile, rinse the rice well in a sieve until the water runs clear. Stir the rice into the broth and bring to a boil. Reduce heat to low, and simmer for 45 to 60 minutes, stirring often, making sure the rice does not stick to the bottom of the pot. Once the rice is the consistency of oatmeal, stir in the chicken and cook for another two minutes. Taste and adjust seasonings.

To make the fried shallots, heat the oil over medium heat until hot. Add the shallots and cook, stirring often until brown and crisp, about 10 minutes. Remove from the pan with a slotted spoon and drain on a paper towel-lined plate.

Ladle the congee into bowls and garnish with fried shallots and optional toppings.

# VEGAN RED CURRY WITH TOFU

## Serves 6-8

This aromatic Thai curry boasts a flavorful medley of vegetables and crispy tofu, all simmered in a perfectly seasoned red curry broth. Its slightly spicy and tangy notes are perfectly balanced by the natural sweetness of coconut milk. This healthy vegan dish is full of nutrients, healthy fats, and plant-based protein, making it a truly satisfying meal. I recommend serving over white rice.

**For the tofu:**
1 (16-ounce) block of firm tofu
1 tablespoon canola oil
1 tablespoon soy sauce
1 tablespoon cornstarch

**Fort the curry:**
2 tablespoons olive or coconut oil
1 red onion, chopped (about 1 cup)
1-inch ginger, grated (about 2 teaspoons)
3 garlic cloves, minced
1 red bell pepper, thinly sliced
1 yellow bell pepper, thinly sliced
1 cup broccoli florets
3 carrots, peeled and sliced on the diagonal
    into ¼-inch thick rounds (about 1 cup)
2 tablespoons Thai red curry paste
1 (15-ounce) can of coconut milk
2 tablespoons low-sodium soy sauce or tamari
½ cup vegetable stock
1 tablespoon coconut or raw sugar
10 leaves of Thai basil, thinly sliced
Juice of 1 lime

**For the tofu:**
Preheat the oven to 400 degrees and line a baking sheet with parchment paper. Place tofu on a paper towel-lined baking sheet. Cover with another layer of paper towels and place a heavy pot on top. Let sit for 30 minutes. Cut into 1-inch cubes.

Transfer the pressed tofu to a medium-sized mixing bowl and drizzle with oil and soy sauce or tamari. Toss to combine. Sprinkle the cornstarch over the tofu and toss the tofu until evenly coated.

Spread on a prepared baking sheet in an even layer and bake for 25 to 30 minutes, tossing the tofu halfway, until the tofu is golden on the edges. Set aside.

**For the curry:**
Heat oil in a large pot over medium heat. Add the onion and cook until soft and translucent, about 6 minutes. Add the ginger and garlic and sauté for another two minutes. Add the bell peppers, broccoli, and carrots. Cook until soft, about 5 minutes, stirring occasionally. Then add the curry paste and cook, stirring often, for 2 minutes. Add the coconut milk, soy sauce or tamari, broth, and sugar, and cook for another 10 minutes. Add the tofu, stir, and simmer for another 3 minutes. Turn off the heat and add the basil and lime juice. Taste and adjust seasonings and serve immediately on its own or over rice.

# COMFORT

# MUSHROOM SOUP

## Serves 6

Earthy and satisfying, this mushroom soup is perfect for the fall and winter months. Mushrooms are a nutrient-rich food, providing an array of health benefits. They enhance immunity, reduce inflammation, and promote heart health. You can use any mushroom variety for this recipe, and if you prefer a lighter version, feel free to omit the cream.

2 tablespoons unsalted butter

2 onions, diced

2 garlic cloves, minced

2 pounds mushrooms (mixed white and brown), sliced

2 teaspoons fresh thyme leaves

½ cup dry white wine

¼ cup all-purpose flour (gluten-free works fine)

1 teaspoon salt

Freshly ground black pepper

3 cups chicken or vegetable stock

¾ cup half and half, cream or crème fraîche (optional)

1 tablespoon fresh lemon juice

2 tablespoons freshly chopped Italian parsley

Melt butter in a large pot over medium-high heat. Add onion and sauté until soft and translucent, about 5 minutes. Add garlic and cook for another minute. Add mushrooms and thyme, and cook for 5 minutes, stirring often. Add wine and cook for 3 minutes.

Sprinkle mushrooms with flour, salt and ¼ teaspoon of fresh black pepper and cook for 2 minutes, stirring frequently. Add stock and bring to a boil. Reduce heat to low, and simmer gently for 15 minutes, until soup thickens.

Remove 1 to 2 cups of the soup and blend in a blender until smooth. Return the blended soup to the pot, stir in the half and half, cream, or crème fraîche, if using, then simmer for another 5 minutes. Remove from heat and add lemon juice. Taste and adjust seasonings if necessary.

Ladle into soup bowls and garnish with chopped parsley.

# MOM'S CHICKEN IN THE POT

Serves 6-8

When I was growing up, my mom's "chicken in the pot" was a household fixture. Although it was essentially just chicken soup with egg noodles, it held a special place in our home. The reason being, my mom would spend days creating the most flavorful and rich stock imaginable. And it's true, the key to a great chicken noodle soup lies in homemade stock. Additionally, she would cut the noodles into bite-sized pieces to make them easier to enjoy with a spoon and always cooked them separately to prevent the starch from altering the stock's flavor. Personally, I enjoy adding a touch of dill to my soup, but my brother thinks that's highly offensive.

1 tablespoon olive oil

1 large onion, diced

2 large carrots, peeled and diced

2 ribs celery ribs, diced

4 garlic cloves, minced

8 cups chicken stock

2 pounds boneless skinless
    chicken thighs or breasts

5 ounces egg noodles or noodles of choice,
    cut into quarters

Salt and pepper, to taste

2 tablespoons chopped fresh parsley leaves

2 tablespoons chopped fresh dill (optional)

1 tablespoon freshly squeezed lemon juice,
    or more, to taste

Heat olive oil in a large pot over medium-high. Add onion, carrots, and celery and sauté until soft, about 5 minutes. Add garlic and cook for another minute. Add the chicken stock and bring to a simmer. Taste the soup then  the seasoning with salt and pepper. Add the chicken and bring the soup back to a low simmer then partially cover the pot with a lid and cook, stirring a few times, until the chicken is cooked through, about 20 minutes. Transfer the cooked chicken to a plate to cool.

While the chicken is cooling, cook noodles separately according to package directions. You can cook noodles directly in soup, but I think it changes the flavor. Once the chicken is cooled, shred or dice it into bite-size pieces. Season the chicken with salt and pepper to taste.

Add the noodles and chicken to the soup. Remove from heat, add the parsley, dill (if using) and lemon juice. Taste and adjust seasonings. Add lemon juice.

Ladle into soup bowls and garnish with chopped parsley.

# NANA'S BEEF & BARLEY

Serves 6-8

This hearty and flavorsome beef and barley soup was a beloved dish in my grandmother's kitchen. Unfortunately, she passed away when I was only two years old, so I never had the chance to learn her exact recipe. However, this version comes pretty close. Just like my grandmother's soup, it embodies a sense of classic comfort. Packed with wholesome vegetables, tender beef, and plump barley, it provides a satisfying and complete meal in a single bowl. If you prefer a gluten-free option, you can substitute the barley with brown rice.

2 pounds beef chuck roast, cut
    into ¾-inch cubes
Salt
Freshly ground black pepper
1 tablespoon olive oil
2 large carrots, peeled and diced
3 celery ribs, diced
1 yellow onion, diced
3 garlic cloves, minced
2 tablespoons tomato paste
6 cups beef stock
1 tablespoon low-sodium soy sauce
2 teaspoons Worcestershire sauce
2 teaspoons minced fresh thyme,
    or ½ teaspoon dried
1 cup pearl barley
3 tablespoons minced fresh parsley

Pat the beef dry with paper towels and season well with salt and pepper. Heat olive oil in a large heavy pot over medium heat. Working in batches if necessary, add the beef and cook, turning occasionally, until well-browned on all sides. Do not overcrowd the pan. Transfer to a large platter. Add carrots, celery and onion to the pot and sauté for 5 minutes. Add the garlic and tomato paste and cook for another minute.

Add the stock, soy sauce, Worcestershire sauce, thyme, ½ teaspoon salt and ¼ teaspoon of fresh black pepper and bring to a boil. Return the beef to the pot, reduce the heat to low and simmer, covered, for 45 minutes. Add the barley and cook for 30 more minutes, uncovered, until tender. Taste and adjust seasonings.

Ladle soup into bowls and garnish with parsley.

# AFRICAN PEANUT SOUP

## Serves 6-8

Peanut soup, also known as Groundnut Soup, is a popular West African dish, particularly in Ghana. The traditional recipe consists of ground peanuts (or peanut butter) combined with tomato paste and various spices. You can use either creamy or crunchy peanut butter, but be sure to choose one without any added sugar. This soup is vegan and dairy-free, although you can always include shredded chicken if desired. It's definitely a soup worth trying!

2 tablespoons olive oil

1 yellow onion, diced

1 tablespoon minced ginger

1 jalapeño, seeds and ribs removed, diced

3 garlic cloves, minced

1 medium sweet potato, peeled and
    chopped into ½-inch cubes

1 teaspoon salt

Freshly ground black pepper

2 teaspoons cumin

Pinch of cayenne pepper

4 tablespoons tomato paste

4 cups chicken or vegetable stock

1 (15-ounce) can chickpeas, drained and rinsed

¾ cup creamy natural peanut butter
    made with ONLY peanuts and salt
    (crunchy or creamy)

2 cups kale leaves or spinach

2 cups shredded rotisserie chicken (optional)

In a large pot, heat olive oil over medium heat. Add onions and sauté until softened, about 3 to 4 minutes. Add in ginger, jalapeño and garlic and stir until fragrant, about 1 minute. Add the sweet potato, salt, a few grinds of black pepper, cumin, cayenne, and tomato paste and cook for another 2 minutes, stirring, until paste darkens. Add the stock, chickpeas and peanut butter. Bring to a boil and stir until fully combined. Turn the heat down to low and simmer for 15 minutes, until the sweet potatoes are tender.

Add spinach or kale and shredded chicken, if using and cook for another 5 minutes. Taste and adjust seasonings.

Ladle the soup into bowls and top with a scoop of rice, cilantro, chopped peanuts, sriracha and serve immediately.

### *Optional*

Top with cooked brown or
white rice, cilantro, crushed
peanuts, sriracha

..................

# FRENCH ONION SOUP

## Serves 6

Warm and decadent, French onion soup is a quintessential dish in French cuisine. This easy recipe features caramelized onions, a flavorful broth, and croutons topped with melted cheese. When preparing this soup, the key is to take ample time to properly caramelize the onions, unlocking their sweet and savory essence.

**For the croutons:**

½ loaf of Italian bread, cut into ¾-inch cubes

2 tablespoons olive oil

¼ teaspoon salt

**For the soup:**

3 tablespoons butter

4 large yellow onions, peeled, halved lengthwise and thinly sliced

1 teaspoon salt

1 teaspoon sugar

2 garlic cloves, minced

1 cup dry white wine

1 teaspoon Worcestershire sauce

4 cups beef or chicken stock

1 tablespoon fresh thyme (or 1 teaspoon dried)

1 ½ cups grated Gruyère cheese

**For the croutons:**

Preheat the oven to 400 degrees. Line a baking sheet with parchment paper. Place the cubed bread on the prepared baking sheet. Drizzle with the olive oil and sprinkle with the salt. Toss gently until well-combined. Spread the bread cubes out in a single layer on a baking sheet. Bake until golden brown, turning once halfway through cooking. Remove from the oven and set aside.

**For the soup:**

Melt the butter in a large pot over medium-high heat. Add in the onions and sauté, stirring often, until softened, about 15 minutes. Reduce the heat to medium-low, stir in the salt and sugar and cook the onions another 35 minutes, stirring every 5 minutes or so, until onions are caramelized. Add the garlic and cook until fragrant, about 1 minute.

Pour in the wine to deglaze the pot, scraping up any brown bits on the bottom and sides. Add in the Worcestershire sauce, stock, and thyme. Gently simmer over low heat for about 20 minutes, stirring occasionally.

To serve, ladle the soup into individual oven safe bowls or one large casserole dish. Cover with croutons and sprinkle with cheese. Put into the broiler for 5 minutes, watching very carefully to avoid burning, until the cheese bubbles and is slightly browned. Serve immediately.

# POTATO LEEK

Serves 6-8

Potato leek soup is a classic for a reason. With its simplicity and comforting flavors, this recipe brings together the delicate combination of potatoes, leeks, and broth, resulting in a velvety and creamy purée. I enjoy garnishing the soup with crispy potato chips, fresh chives, and a touch of hot sauce for an extra burst of flavor.

2 tablespoons unsalted butter

3 large leeks, white and light green parts only, roughly chopped and rinsed

3 garlic cloves, chopped

2 pounds Yukon Gold potatoes, peeled and roughly chopped into 1-inch pieces

4 cups chicken or vegetable stock

4 sprigs fresh thyme or ¾ teaspoon dried thyme

1 teaspoon salt

¼ teaspoon ground black pepper

½ cup sour cream

¼ cup heavy cream

Melt the butter In a large pot over medium-high heat. Add in the leeks and sauté, stirring often, until softened, about 6 minutes. Add garlic and cook for another minute. Add the chopped potato, stock, thyme, salt, pepper, and bring to a simmer. Simmer for 20 minutes until the potatoes are tender. Remove the thyme stems.

Remove from heat and carefully pour the soup mixture into a Vitamix or high-powered blender and blend until smooth, taking care when blending hot liquids. Return the soup to a clean pot.

Add the sour cream and cream. Taste and adjust seasonings as desired. Ladle the soup into bowls and top with fresh chives, potato chips and a dash of hot sauce, if desired.

### Optional

Top with chives, potato chips, hot sauce

...................

# SLOW COOKER
# CREAMY CHICKEN & WILD RICE

Serves 6-8

This satisfying soup is the ultimate cozy comfort food for a cold winter day. The combination of tender chicken, nutty wild rice, and a rich creamy broth is completely comforting and flavorful. An added bonus is that it is made in the slow cooker, which saves time and makes clean-up easy.

1 cup wild rice

1 pound boneless, skinless chicken breast

1 yellow onion, diced

2 large carrots, peeled and diced

3 celery ribs, diced

3 garlic cloves, minced

1 bay leaf

¼ teaspoon dried thyme

¼ teaspoon dried sage

¼ teaspoon dried rosemary

4 cups chicken stock

1 teaspoon salt

Freshly ground black pepper

4 tablespoons butter

½ cup all-purpose flour

1 ½ cups milk

½ cup heavy cream

Rinse the rice well. Combine chicken, onions, carrots, celery, garlic, bay leaf, uncooked rice, chicken stock, dried herbs, salt and ¼ teaspoon of fresh black pepper in the slow cooker. Cover and set on high for 4 hours. In the last 30 minutes of cooking, remove the chicken from the slow cooker and let cool slightly. Once cool enough to handle, shred chicken with your hands or two forks and add back to the slow cooker. Remove the bay leaf and discard.

Melt the butter in a small saucepan. Add the flour and whisk well for a minute. Continue whisking the mixture while slowly adding the milk. Continue to whisk until the mixture becomes thick and creamy and all the lumps have dissolved. Add the roux into the slow cooker and stir to combine. Add additional water or milk if the soup is too thick. Season with salt and pepper to taste.

# CIOPPINO

Serves 6-8

Cioppino is a hearty, rustic Italian-American fish stew that originated in my hometown of San Francisco. It is typically made with a variety of seafood, such as shrimp, mussels, clams, crab, and fish, all simmered in a tomato-based broth. This Cioppino recipe is perfect for a dinner party or Sunday supper and can be adapted to include any seafood you desire. Traditionally, Cioppino is served with sourdough toast, which is perfect for soaking up all the flavorful broth.

¼ cup olive oil
1 yellow onion, diced
2 medium shallots, diced
1 fennel bulb, cored and diced
4 garlic cloves, minced
2 tablespoons tomato paste
½ teaspoon dried oregano
1 teaspoon salt
¼ teaspoon crushed red pepper flakes
1 cup dry white wine
1 (28-ounce) can crushed tomatoes
4 cups seafood stock
1 bay leaf
1 pound fresh mussels, scrubbed
    and debearded
1 pound fresh clams, scrubbed
1 pound fresh white fish, like cod, halibut
    or sea bass, cut into 2-inch pieces
1 pound shrimp, peeled and deveined
¼ cup fresh chopped parsley
Lemon wedges, for serving
Sourdough bread, for serving

Heat the olive oil in a large pot over medium-high heat. Add the onion, shallot, and fennel and sauté, stirring often, until softened, about 6 minutes. Add the garlic, tomato paste, oregano, salt and red pepper flakes and cook for another minute. Stir in the wine, tomatoes, stock and bay leaf and bring to a boil, reduce heat and simmer and cook for about 20 minutes. Taste and season with salt and pepper if needed.

Stir in clams and mussels. Reduce heat to low. Cover, with a tight-fitting lid, and cook until the clams and mussels are just beginning to open, about 3 to 4 minutes. Stir in cod or halibut and shrimp. Reduce heat and simmer until fish and shrimp are just cooked through and clams and mussels have opened completely, about 3 to 4 minutes. Discard any unopened shellfish. Stir in parsley and serve immediately with the lemon wedges and sourdough bread.

# INDEX

Poblano
  Chicken Pozole Verde 64
Red Bell
  Quinoa Chili 84
  Vegan Red Curry with Tofu 136
Yellow Bell
  Vegan Red Curry with Tofu 136

## Potato
Albóndigas Soup (Mexican Meatball Soup) 78
Potato Leek 152

## Pork
Pork Pozole Rojo 68
Spaghetti & Meatball Soup 41
Wonton Soup 122

## Quinoa
Quinoa Chili 84

## Radish
Asian Chicken Noodle 131
Chicken Pozole Verde 64
Pork Pozole Rojo 68

## Red Curry Paste
Thai Coconut Soup 132
Vegan Red Curry with Tofu 136

## Rice
Brown
  Butternut Squash, Brown Rice
  & Mushroom Soup 89
White
  Albóndigas Soup (Mexican Meatball Soup) 78
  Chicken Congee 135
Wild
  Slow Cooker Creamy Chicken & Wild Rice 155

## Sausage
White Bean, Sausage & Kale Soup 54

## Sesame Oil
Chicken Ramen 118
Wonton Soup 122

## Sesame Seeds
Chicken Ramen 118

## Shallots
Chicken Congee 135
Cioppino 156

Carrot Soup 109
Thai Shrimp Coconut Soup 132

## Shellfish Shells
Seafood Stock 27

## Shrimp
Cioppino 156
Thai Shrimp Coconut Soup 132

## Slow Cooker
Slow Cooker Creamy Chicken and Wild Rice 155
Slow Cooker White Bean Chili 60

## Sriracha
Chicken Ramen 118
Curried Sweet Potato Soup 93

## Sour Cream
Albóndigas Soup (Mexican Meatball Soup) 78
Easy Black Bean Soup 77
Game Day Turkey Black Bean Chili 83
Orange October Chicken Tortilla Soup 73
Potato Leek 152
Quinoa Chili 84
Slow Cooker White Bean Chili 60

## Soy Sauce
Asian Chicken Noodle 131
Chicken Ramen 118
Vegan Red Curry with Tofu 136
Wonton Soup 122

## Spices
Bay Leaves
  Beef Stock 26
  Chicken Pozole Verde 64
  Chicken Stock 25
  Cioppino 156
  Pork Pozole Rojo 68
  Ribollita 37
  Slow Cooker Creamy Chicken & Wild Rice 155
  Vegetable Stock 27
Cayenne
  African Peanut Soup 147
  Easy Black Bean Soup 77
  Quinoa Chili 84
Chili Powder
  Albóndigas Soup (Mexican Meatball Soup) 78
  Game Day Turkey Black Bean Chili 83
  Orange October Chicken Tortilla Soup 73
  Quinoa Chili 84

Slow Cooker White Bean Chili 60
Cinnamon stick
   Pho 126
Cloves
   Pho 126
Coriander
   Pho 126
Cumin
   African Peanut Soup 147
   Albóndigas Soup (Mexican Meatball Soup) 78
   Chicken Pozole Verde 64
   Curried Sweet Potato Soup 93
   Easy Black Bean Soup 77
   Game Day Turkey Black Bean Chili 83
   Green or Red Lentil Curry 105
   Orange October Chicken Tortilla Soup 73
   Pork Pozole Rojo 68
   Quinoa Chili 84
   Slow Cooker White Bean Chili 60
   Super Green Alkalizing Soup 97
Curry
   Curried Sweet Potato Soup 93
   Green or Red Lentil Curry 105
Oregano
   Albóndigas Soup (Mexican Meatball Soup) 78
   Chicken Pozole Verde 64
   Chicken Tortellini Soup 53
   Cioppino 156
   Orange October Chicken Tortilla Soup 73
   Pork Pozole Rojo 68
   Slow Cooker White Bean Chili 60
Peppercorns
   Beef Stock 26
   Chicken Stock 25
   Pho 126
   Vegetable stock 27
Red Chili Flakes
   Asian Chicken Noodle 131
   Chicken Ramen 118
   Chickpea & Kale Stew 113
   Cioppino 156
   Escarole & White Bean Soup 38
   Ribollita 37
   Tomato Soup No. 2 (Anytime Canned) 49
   White Bean, Sausage and Kale Soup 54
Rosemary
   Slow Cooker Creamy Chicken
   and Wild Rice 155
Sage
   Slow Cooker Creamy Chicken
   and Wild Rice 155
Star anise
   Pho 126

Thyme
   Beef Stock 26
   Chicken Tortellini Soup 53
   French Onion Soup 148
   Mushroom Soup 140
   Nana's Beef & Barley 144
   Potato Leek 152
   Seafood Stock 27
   Slow Cooker Creamy Chicken
   & Wild Rice 155
Turmeric
   Curried Sweet Potato Soup 93
   Green or Red Lentil Curry 105
   Thai Shrimp Coconut Soup 132

Spinach
   Chicken Tortellini Soup 53
   Detox Lentil & Split Pea Soup 94
   Italian Wedding Soup 35
   Super Green Alkalizing Soup 97
   Spring Green Minestrone with Pesto 102
   Tuscan Farro Soup 57

Split peas
   Detox Lentil & Split Pea Soup 94

Stock
   Beef Stock 26
   Chicken Stock 25
   Seafood Stock 27
   Vegetable Stock  27

Sweet Potato
   African Peanut Soup 147
   Curried Sweet Potato Soup 93

Tomatillos
   Chicken Pozole Verde 64

Tomato paste
   African Peanut Soup 147
   Beef Stock 26
   Nana's Beef & Barley 144
   Seafood Stock 27
   Summer Minestrone 41
   White Bean, Sausage & Kale Soup 54

Tomatoes
   Albóndigas Soup (Mexican Meatball Soup) 78
   Chickpea & Kale Stew 113
   Cioppino 156
   Game Day Turkey Black Bean Chili 83
   Orange October Chicken Tortilla Soup 73

# WITH GRATITUDE

After writing *Salad Love*, I never thought I would be publishing a second cookbook, let alone one year later! But, here I am and feeling so grateful. I can't thank all of my supporters enough. It was without a doubt your big love for *Salad Love* that inspired me to do it again. All of your emails, texts, instagram messages and positive feedback gave me the energy and confidence to write this book. I hope you find *Soup Love* as useful and inspiring as *Salad Love*.

Soup is incredibly meaningful to me and I wanted the book to impart that sentiment. Thanks to my outstanding creative team, this is more than a book of soup recipes, it is a reflective, sentimental and personal cookbook. For a week, we shot the entire book at my home in San Francisco. We cooked, we laughed, we ate LOTS of soup, read tarot cards, and created. Michelle Min and assistant Cory Maryott did their magic behind the camera. Thanks to them, every beautiful photo tells a story that fully captures each soup. Food stylist, Fanny Pan, and prop stylist, Lizzie Oh, dressed up my soups and made them look prettier than I ever knew was possible. And finally, Allison Fellion helped me in the kitchen...chopping, lifting, and lots and lots of stirring. All of your creative energy, passion and teamwork are truly inspirational.

Thank you to Christian Reynoso for editing and cleaning up my imperfect writing. If you find any grammatical errors, blame him.

And the best for last. Alyssa Warnock, I am eternally grateful to you for bringing my book to life. Everything you touch turns to gold and I have no doubt that your warm and welcoming design will make *Soup Love* approachable and loved by all.